MANY DOORS

By Pauline Meller

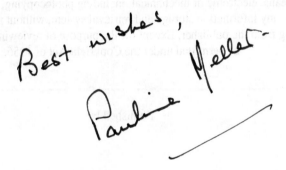

Best wishes,

Pauline Meller

CON-PSY PUBLICATIONS MIDDLESEX

First Edition
2001

©Pauline Meller

Published by

CON-PSY PUBLICATIONS

P.O. BOX 14,
GREENFORD,
MIDDLESEX, UB6 0UF.

ISBN 1 898680 24 8

CONTENTS

Events depicted are true. Names and places are mainly fictional.

PROLOGUE

It was a lovely clear, warm, sunny day and I was feeling very regal, perched alone in the dickie seat of the high, open motor car. It had been quite a scramble up the step over the rear wheel and following mother's instructions, I had been careful not to dirty my best dress. The day promised to be a happy one and I could only guess at the treats in store. To be out alone with my favourite aunt and uncle was something really special, and I loved outings in this car. There was something about the leathery smell of the upholstery and the bright, shiny brass motor horn that always excited me.

Aunt and uncle didn't have children of their own. Their nieces and nephew filled the gap and they enjoyed taking us on day trips through the Kentish lanes, down to Sussex and Eastbourne, Brighton or other south coast resorts, or perhaps eastwards to Margate or Clacton. These day trips were really special, but they were usually family affairs. My younger sister Joan would sit between aunt and uncle in the front, and my parents and I would sit in the dickie with my small brother on mum's lap. Now I had a new baby sister and if I thought about it at all, would have guessed that mum was too busy to come along. But I was just too happy to wonder where the others were or what they were doing. It was all very exciting and I was enjoying being allowed out without them.

I suppose I was a normal eleven year old but being the eldest child a good deal was expected of me and inwardly I considered myself quite grown up. Today felt special and without the family I saw myself as really independent and adult. The country road down which we drove was beautiful. Late spring flowers grew in profusion. I recognised poppies but there were other unnamed yellow and blue flowers growing prettily in the hedgerows with a scattering of daisies here and there. I marvelled at the clear light and bright sunshine dappling through tall trees which gracefully bent inwards to almost form an archway over our heads. It did not strike me as strange that there was a limit to my vision. Of the surrounding countryside I could see nothing.

Suddenly we were confronted by high, black wrought iron gates such as I had only previously seen leading into a London park. But as we approached they slowly swung open to let us drive through. We were now in a lane and the sunlight had gone. It seemed then that my aunt and uncle became remote and removed from me. Although they were still in the car it was as though I was alone and when I saw the first body I was unable to call out or communicate with them. They certainly did not seem to be aware of anything unusual but sat woodenly looking straight ahead.

In a flash of insight and panic, I suddenly knew why we were there. I was searching for my mother and father among the corpses that were now lying along the right-hand side of the lane. Anxiously I scanned the scene as uncle drove slowly past. But there was no sign of my parents. The real horror began when, a little further on, I saw brown corpses. Naked and withered corpses, here twisted and distorted, there laid out straight and stiff, some piled high, others so entangled with each other that identification was impossible. The horror was indescribable, but I could not turn away. I had to go on searching. The responsibility for finding my parents was mine and mine alone. I did not get out of the car but sat transfixed as we motored slowly on and on. In a strange way my uncle and aunt remained uninvolved. It was as though there was a solid invisible screen between us.

I continued my fruitless search for what seemed an interminable time until it suddenly became too much to bear. In my despair I awoke, in my own bed, trembling and frightened. Afraid to go back to sleep I lay reluctantly replaying this strange dream and in my distress found it hard to believe that my parents were in fact, asleep in the next room. It did not occur to me to wake them. Their bedroom was strictly out of bounds. And so the seeds of my independence and self-reliance were nurtured and flourished.

It was the beginning of a nightmare existence. By day I went to school where I was considered a bright pupil and my parents had great hopes for me. But I was lively, impatient and too easily distracted. I excelled in those subjects which interested me, but did poorly where the teaching was slack and the class disruptive. It was not unknown for me to welcome such diversions and I was usually happy to join in the chaos that ensued.

At home I was a gay, cheerful child always singing and dancing around the house and forever reading books and any scrap of print that came to hand. But essentially I was also a compliant child, the eldest and "little mother" to my sister and brother who were entrusted to my care when I came home at teatime. Discipline was strict and we lived by predictable routines carried over from mother's own childhood in the Edwardian period before the First World War. We were often reminded that children were to be seen but not heard, and I was always being told to be quiet and go away and find something to do. Joan and I had our regular chores around the house, and meals were formal family affairs with strict observance to table manners, after which Joan and I would wash and dry the dishes. No dishwashers then!

Summer or winter the rule was bed at 7.30, but we would read and often talk until all light had faded from the room. But I could not confide in her or anyone else the apprehension and dread I faced every night. Even at that age I knew without a shadow of doubt that it would have been wrong to frighten her as I myself was afraid. My mother was fully occupied with baby Valerie, and I knew, or thought I knew, that she would have dismissed my dreams as childish nightmares and would probably have said that I was reading too much.

So it was that night after night an overwhelming and solitary dread gripped me and kept me awake until long after everyone else in the house was asleep and the summer nights had faded into darkness. Always the dream was exactly the same. The eager anticipation of an outing in the car to the countryside I loved. The joy of freedom, the sunlight playing through the branches of the trees which almost closed overhead, and the high wide gates opening before us onto the sombre lane and the horrors beyond. The awful sight of the naked and skeletal bodies and the frantic, desperate, never ending search for my parents. The details never varied. The pressure and obligation to find them were too much for a child of eleven. But in my dream I never questioned why my aunt and uncle were not concerned in the search. All I knew, with the utmost certainty, was that the responsibility to find them was mine. It was strange that I never travelled to the end of the lane neither did I complete my search before fear and distress awoke me. It was then that I lay awake tossing and turning, afraid to sleep in case it would all begin again.

The nightmare in all its squalor haunted me. My thoughts often flicked back to it during the day and I dreaded bedtime. It was almost a week before I had a sound nights sleep, probably from exhaustion. From then on it became repetitive, first a few times a week, then spacing out until first a week and later a month would pass without a reoccurrence. I would grow to think that it had left me only to have a disturbing replay after several months and then even after a year and then another year and another year. Later, it took me a long time to realise that it had mercifully gone forever.

In 1945, some thirteen years after the first dream, I visited a cinema and saw the first newsreel of the liberation of a German concentration camp by Allied Forces. There was my nightmare! The dreadful details were exactly as I had seen them so many times. I could not understand what I was seeing. How could I have witnessed the bestial horrors of the extermination camps years before they had even occurred? I sat transfixed and solitary in the darkened cinema appalled, stunned and shaken by an overwhelming sense of de-ja vu.

CHAPTER 1 - SPITTLEFIELDS

Events happen in life which at the time seem unremarkable, but in fact, may have an extraordinary affect on our future. A casual meeting, remark or conversation may open a door leading to new employment, a new way of life, or even whole new ways of thought. There are many occasions when doors of opportunity are presented to us but we do not recognise them for what they are, or if we do, decide to pass them by. It may be that careers or personal circumstances appear at the time to be more important, and prevent us from pursuing a potentially new opening. The choice is always ours and we have the freedom of action to explore or ignore that which is before us. There are times when prejudice or preconceived ideas stand between us and an open door and it should be recognised that an open mind is the surest passport of entry to an open door and all that lies beyond.

It was such a door that opened for me in 1938 when, out of curiosity, I found myself attending a Spiritualist church. It had come about through a casual invitation from two girls who worked in the same office as myself. One had paid a previous visit to a seance which she had found interesting but so unusual that she was keen to get someone else's opinion. Casually and quite light heartedly, without any thought except that it might be something "different", I agreed to join them.

So it was that on a bright spring evening we set off for Spittlefields which at that time, was a seedy area of tenements, old houses and prostitution. In its heyday it had been the silk weaving centre of London, built round the ancient church of St Bartholomew The Great. Now its fame resided in the adjacent wholesale fruit, vegetable and flower market. The meeting was to be held in an upstairs room of one of the old buildings and the medium, Joseph Benjamin was of course, unknown to me, and anyway not yet the renowned person he was later to become. A few years down the road it would be difficult to get into his meetings, such was his high reputation and popularity. At the time, and in the months that followed I did not recognise his special qualities neither did I realise how very fortunate I was to be initiated into the "ism" through such a gifted clairvoyant.

There were about thirty people, mainly women, already seated on wooden chairs when we arrived and were shown into a middle row. The proceedings opened with a short prayer after which the congregation sang a hymn without a piano or other musical accompaniment. Even after all these years, I never hear "Nearer My God To Thee" without being transported back to relive the expectancy that was palpable in the gradually darkening room. There then followed a demonstration of clairvoyance by the medium who allegedly transmitted messages from relatives and friends who had died. The messages were pictorially detailed and appeared to be fully acceptable to the recipients.

It was unexpected, on that first evening, to be singled out by the medium who told me that I would soon be changing my job and to go ahead as it would be a very good move. This was embarrassing as my office colleagues didn't know that only a few days earlier I had taken steps towards obtaining a new position, and I had to make light of it and laughed it off. But secretly I was impressed! How could he possibly know? Was this message really from someone who was a "spirit" or might it be telepathy, or perhaps, something entirely different? Whatever, it seemed quite remarkable to me and presented me with a door I knew I wanted to explore.

When I got home and told Mother about the intriguing events of the evening, she confounded me by saying that my uncle, her brother Jim, was a practising Spiritual healer, and although grandma knew, it was not talked about in the family. It appeared that he was longstanding member of the local church in his home town some thirty miles from London, and had built up a good local reputation for the success of his healing work. From the perspective that he was the jolliest of my mother's five brothers, the life and soul of any party, I came to the conclusion that Spittlefields was probably not so weird after all. After that night mum, who was curious about the concept of life after death, accompanied me and we became regular members of the small congregation.

Most weeks, after the room had gradually darkened, Joseph Benjamin would retire to a corner of the L-shaped room, away from view of the sitters, to prepare for direct voice communication with those who had 'died'. At this time the congregation would be holding hands and quietly singing hymns, usually starting with "Open Mine Eyes", a beautiful hymn which set a tone of reverence for what was to come. Then a voice from the darkened recess would speak and someone among the congregation would recognise the voice and exclaim "That's my little girl" or perhaps "That's mother" and go forward to hold a conversation with their loved one. We were told this was made possible through the mediumship of Joseph Benjamin and the use of his vocal apparatus by spirit guides. The atmosphere was highly charged and the grateful tears of those fortunate to have such conversations helped to persuade me that something very special was taking place. Something quite beyond my comprehension.

Whilst all this was happening away from the main part of the room, a healing session would be held where we were sitting. Two lady healers identified those whom they considered needed their help, although it was also possible to ask for healing. One occasion, without any prompting from me, a healer asked me to go forward which I readily agreed to do. For some time I had been suffering pains which had been medically diagnosed as a 'grumbling appendix' and had spent ten days in hospital on a special diet, to relieve it. The healing that night, consisted of nothing more than a few light passes of the healer's hands across the lower part of my stomach and at the time, I had no sensation of anything special happening. Nevertheless, the healing was successful and I had immediate relief from the nagging discomfort.

I was not totally convinced that all "messages" came from loved ones who have passed on to the higher life. Some, I felt sure, although given in good faith, might have another source. It seemed to me at the time, that if something was occupying ones mind it might possibly be picked up mentally by a person with the gift of telepathy. So I was somewhat confused. But some of my confusion was stilled when weeks, then months, then years passed without even a twinge of pain and I realised that I had experienced my first personal proof of the power of Spiritual healing. From that time on, I have never doubted its reality. I have known it to be successful not only in psychosomatic illnesses and those which are stress related, but also in conditions of the bones, vital organs, eyesight and hearing. It is unfortunate that sufferers often resort to spiritual healing and other natural healing techniques, only as a last resort. They may accept that the medical profession can do little more for them, and yet still feel cheated if they don't find a miracle cure at the hands of unorthodox practitioners. Experience has shown that it is not within a healer's power to determine who will or will not be cured, although a healer with a powerful healing guide will always bring about a betterment in one form or another and to a lesser or greater degree.

Our experience at Spittlefields did not conflict with our religious beliefs at home where under our parents' guidance, God played a natural part in our lives. We accepted the supremacy of His Will in all that we did and aspired to do. From a very early age mother taught us "You appoint and the Almighty disappoints". From this we understood that He was not being cruel or unkind but rather that He knew what was best for us and was very much involved in our lives. In hindsight I can see how this helped assuage our disappointment when she refused us something we dearly would have liked to have had! But it instilled in us a philosophical outlook where we became strong in spirit and accepted the variegations in life as normal and bearable.

Although both my parents were born Jewish, dad's views were unconventional and free-thinking. He regarded all men as the sons of God and taught us that by prayer we had a "direct line" to the Almighty. As a regular soldier and an Old Contemptible of the First World War, he was sympathetic to conscripted men of all armies, realising they had little choice but to fight. His disillusionment with religion had its roots in the fact that clergy of all denominations, on both sides of the conflict, urged men into battle and the horrors of No-man's Land, assuring them that God and Right was on their side. This was difficult to reconcile with his upbringing or the Christian ethic of love and charity.

Under his influence we accepted the Darwinian theory of man's physical evolution and regarded the bible as a combination of history, fables and moral teachings. It was quite commonplace for dad and I to sit up all hours in debate and discussion. We ranged over thorny aspects of religion, politics – not surprisingly he was left of centre – and being on the threshold of new communication technology he had visions of the new future, a great deal of which he blessedly lived to see come to fruition. Although we were both strong minded, he was instrumental in encouraging me to be independent in thought, value freedom of expression, and indeed, to stand as an individual for what I believe to be right.

As a typical teenager there was much confusion in my mind. There were so many questions I wanted to have answered. What, I mused, is life all about? Why are we born? Why are we here? What does it all mean? What is the purpose of it all? Why is it so important that we should always be honest and truthful, never go back on our given word, be responsible and not let other people down? I understood about trying to be kind and helpful and putting other peoples' needs before our own, but it did not answer the question of why we should always do what is regarded as being right, even though it may involve considerable inconvenience or difficulties for ourselves. I confess to wondering if it all really mattered as long as we were doing our best? It did not occur to me to ask if my best was good enough!

But through my visits to Spittlefields I came to accept that an afterlife probably existed. If true it would make some sense in light of the questions bothering me. But my father would have none of it. He had seen too much warfare. Too many men obliterated to be able to accept that any part of them could still exist. For him death was final and in spite of our coaxing to come with us to a meeting, he was adamant in his refusal. In our opinion he was being obstinate and intolerant. In his eyes we were being gullible and naive. It was one argument I just could not win!

These early experiences encouraged me to think that perhaps death was not the end and that we might continue to live after we "die". If this were so, perhaps communication between those here and those who had passed on, could actually take place. I had experienced the effectiveness of Spiritual healing and recognised that to be able to relieve pain must involve a power for good. I was inclined to think that the spirit 'messages' I had heard and experienced, probably or possibly, came from the same source. But beyond that my knowledge was limited and I knew little more than I have shown. At that time it was sufficient for me to believe in the existence of a supreme loving power whom we call God and I felt that everything I had seen and heard at Spittlefields was part of God's work.

My knowledge and experience of personal guides and helpers and the interaction between the spirit realms and our own, did not come until many years later and then only by degrees. An account of the gradual discovery of my own psychic ability which developed parallel to an equally gradual development of spiritual awareness, and has led to a measure of spiritual progression, is the theme of this book. It is being written in the hope that it may help others on a similar pathway of discovery.

There are so many people whose thoughts, prompted by their deeply hidden spiritual consciousness, take them beyond the parameters of conventional religious doctrine. They often feel isolated and even a little odd, believing there are no others around to share their ideas and embryonic philosophy. They recognise that there must be more to life than the daily grind. And more to life than discos, holidays and other pleasures which are the material rewards of a material world. They may recognise that these pleasures, whilst enjoyable at the time, have little lasting value. When the holiday is over and the party finished, it is easy to slip into discontent and a yearning for something deeper.

But there are thousands and thousands of others who feel the same spiritual hunger and search for a doorway to lead them into understanding that there is far more to life than appears. They have yet to realise that the unseen is more real than that which appears to have substance, but being material, is transient and will often let us down.

CHAPTER 2 – UNWELCOME VISITOR

The beginning of the Second World War put an end to our visits to Spittlefields. Life changed for everyone over the next few years. Most of the population, certainly all the young people, were uprooted and directed into new surroundings where they met people and situations outside their normal experience and lifestyle. Thousands in the armed forces were subjected to hardship and danger beyond their imagination, and countless others had to adapt to working in factories, coal mines and on the land. But it was not all discomfort and adversity. In those eventful times life quickened as young people realised there may not be many tomorrows. Life had to be lived to the full. In the new found freedom life became exciting, friendships easily made, and love was urgent and compelling. It was the older generation who had already lived through the First World War and experienced its horrors, who were most anxious and apprehensive, fearing the future and the wiping out of another generation of the nation's young men.

In the field of employment it had become apparent that I quickly became bored once a particular job or routine had been mastered. Full of confidence, I was ever ready to explore new grounds and new challenges, and in the process of moving from job to job gained wider than usual experience of office routines. Early in the war our home in London fell casualty to the bombing and the family unexpectedly found itself living in Gloucestershire. For almost a year I ran the library in a local bookshop, and then Joan and I obtained employment in the offices of a factory making guidance instruments for the R.A.F. This was classified as essential work and meant we were safe from being conscripted into the armed forces or Land Army. But it was the attraction of doing something different and adventurous, which persuaded us to leave our safe "reserved" positions, and join the army. We both served almost four years in the London area, but that is another story!

Joan and I served on heavy anti-aircraft sites in the battery offices until our paths split and for a brief spell I found myself with the battery of anti-aircraft guns in Hyde Park. Winston Churchill's daughter Mary, a generous and charming subaltern was in an adjoining office. Word came that I had been selected to go on special duties involving top secret work and promotion - an exciting prospect. However, before it materialised another posting came through and I found myself among a group forming new army headquarters at a secret address in west London. The promotion prospects were good but I blocked my chances by trying to persuade the powers that be that I should not be there. For a month I lazed the time away on the cricket pitch working up a good suntan in the wonderful summer of 1943, until I was told that the first posting had fallen through and the job I had been posted to at the new headquarters had now been filled. They did not know what to do with me which is how I found myself temporarily occupying a desk in an office with a very quiet young draughtsman who was always engrossed in his work and barely seemed to notice me.

But I could not fail to notice him. His natural grace, reserve and good manners were in contrast to the general ruggedness I had met in so many other young men. Ron had a refinement that set him apart, and when we eventually talked I found in him a sincerity and wisdom far beyond his twenty-two years. I felt he was someone I could trust, someone who would be reliable and upon whom I could depend. We started going out and about with a regular small group of friends and we were all charmed and amused by his sharp wit and good humour. We spent our days off visiting theatres and cinemas so abundant in London's West End. And I taught him to dance. He was graceful and stylish and dancing became our favourite past-time for the next fifty three years.

It was a whirlwind courtship which confounded our friends who thought we were too dissimilar to find lasting happiness. In many ways we were opposites who complemented each other. Quick and slow, impetuous and thoughtful, extravagance and caution, and where I would act on intuition he required time, sometimes days, to consider facts. When in later years I asked him why he had married me, he replied quite simply, "Because I saw the good in you." At the time it seemed an ambiguous reply and it has taken almost a lifetime for me to understand that we had recognised each other on a spiritual level above our normal consciousness. We married eight months after we first met; just before the army sent him to Europe.

I take up my story again in 1945 when after demobilisation, I went to a town in the Midlands to live with my mother-in-law and await Ron's return to this country and his longed for release from the services. It was a time of high hopes and anticipation when every ex-serviceman and woman was looking forward to making a new life. In my case the immediate reality was quite different from that which I had anticipated. I had only met my mother-in-law twice before getting married and quite unexpectedly, and without prior warning, I found myself living with a sad, neurotic woman whose sole preoccupation was her husband's desertion and the resulting divorce.This had happened some twelve years earlier but was still her main and almost only, topic of conversation. She was completely obsessed and unable to get on with her life. In her misery she had allowed herself to be eaten up by bitterness and recriminations. Today, there no longer being stig-

13

ma attached to divorce, she would have been able to receive sympathetic counselling through the medical profession and various agencies. Or perhaps, she may have allowed herself to be helped by spiritual healing which could have induced a calmer state of mind. And no doubt, during healing sessions she would have received counselling encouraging her to open her heart and mind to forgiveness and release the bitterness that ruled her. But she was isolated in her unhappiness.

I wasn't a patient person at the best of times, but I can honestly say that I tried to cope although the situation was quite alien to me. It was the first time in my young life that I had come face to face with such negative attitudes. My home life had been strict but it was loving and although we argued and bickered, it was without rancour or malice and I had no experience of antagonism and vindictiveness. To my consternation I discovered that her antagonism even extended to me, as I was seen as the person who had come between her and her dreams for the future which had been built around Ron, her only son who remained at home. The interminable harping on one subject and the constant tears affected me so that I felt trapped in a situation beyond my control. After a few months it came to the point when it was more than I could handle and I left.

I did not have the awareness to understand that under spirit influence I was being guided out of a depressing and negative situation which could have adversely affected my very being. It was only much later when I learned that we are what we think, and that our thoughts today fashion the person we become tomorrow, that I realised how right it had been for me to leave. This episode and the one that immediately followed, proved to be important staging posts along my life's pathway, and were the first intimation I had that bad times and experiences often lead to unimaginable good fortune and happiness.

My father-in-law was a totally different person and doubtless my parents-in-law had been an ill matched couple. He was a tall, slim, educated man, soft voiced with a kind, gentle nature. In fact, he was an older version of my husband and it was not difficult to turn to him for help. I 'phoned him and was invited out to dinner to talk things over. In the quiet atmosphere of a small restaurant he listened sympathetically to my situation, and I appreciated that he was the one person who could readily understand the conditions I had walked away from.

Although naturally reserved and cautious and not given to extravagant gestures, he nevertheless kindly came to my rescue by offering to let me live in his town house whilst he was living in the countryside with his present wife. It was a wonderful solution to my problems and I gratefully accepted on the basis that I would move out when they wished to move

14

back to town. Which was how I found myself occupying a half furnished, nine roomed, three storey house. The fact that the house was cold and sombre was not surprising as it had stood virtually empty most of the war years. But I chose to ignore the disadvantages as it was a relief to be alone, away from the depleting environment of recent months.

Across the top of the house was a large billiard room, whilst in the basement was an extensive cellar. On the floors between were four bedrooms, two of which were unfurnished, sitting room, dining room, study and kitchen, all linked by three flights of stairs. The longest flight led from the ground floor to the first and was situated so that when ascending one's back was turned to the door of the billiard room above. It was always unnerving to go up to bedrooms on the first floor as it was impossible to escape the uncanny feeling of being observed by someone standing in the doorway above. The stare seemed to penetrate and prickle the back of my head, but when I turned to look up there was never anyone there. Only once I climbed the top flight and ventured into the room. I found it contained a billiard table, chairs and various storage boxes but it was icy cold and I wasn't brave enough to stay.

After moving into my new accommodation I made it a priority to find permanent employment that would lead to a fulfilling career. I had several offers locally, but eventually accepted a post on the other side of town. In addition to private secretarial duties I was employed as Welfare and Personnel Officer for the female staff of a group of five small engineering companies. It was a responsible interesting job with no two days alike, and there was no doubt that I had found my ideal occupation. A bonus came in the form of two good new friendships. Rita was a director's private secretary and Norma was chief cook in charge of the group's canteens. Although I saw more of Rita as she lived near to me, Norma and I also had a great deal in common as she too, had served in the A.T.S. and we sometimes visited each other at the weekend or went into town shopping.

There was one particular evening when Rita and I went to see the latest Hollywood film that the programme also included the first newsreel of the liberation of a concentration camp in Europe. The horror and revulsion which was shared by all who saw it was, in my case, compounded by the fact that I had seen it all before. I sat there stunned and speechless, washed over by so many emotions of which incredulity was paramount. How could I have seen the events – and in such detail – so many years before? I went home troubled not knowing what to make of it. I had no answers although I eventually came to question whether there might be a connection between my experience and the predictions into the future given by Joseph Benjamin at Spittlefields.

Housing was a difficult problem after the war. Bombing had taken its toll, women had often returned to their parental home, and no new housing had been built. The little accommodation there was available commanded high rents. Most landlords took advantage of the situation and insisted that prospective tenants purchase inferior carpets, armchairs and other bits and pieces of furniture. In this way the property acquired legal status as furnished accommodation which was favourable to the landlord. At the same time they were charging premiums for keys to the property. Moving was an expensive and frustrating business, often beyond the pockets of ex-service personnel. So although I knew my new accommodation was temporary and not a long term solution, I was very grateful to my father-in-law for giving me a home.

It became normal for him to come to the house twice a week to pick up his mail and take me into town for dinner. They were pleasant evenings which I looked forward to, and I am sure it pleased him to have a young, personable girl on his arm. In short, we enjoyed each others company. The house however, continued to feel chilly, even unwelcoming. It needed to be fully furnished and warmth brought into its walls. It needed a family to live in it and laugh in it. As it was, I found it difficult to be really comfortable and when I went out with my father-in-law or friends, I contrived to return as late as possible before settling down to write my daily letter to Ron, and then it would be time for bed.

It was one night, some months after my arrival, when I had written my letter and was just settling down to sleep in my first floor bedroom, that I heard footsteps coming up the stairs. There were various creaks and sounds in the old house, but there was no mistaking the fact that these were footsteps. Immediately I was alert and anxious. Listening intently I sensed the bedroom door opening – but there was no sound. In the eerie silence I half lifted my head and peered towards the foot of the bed. My heart pounded in my throat, as there in the light of the window stood a figure. It was impossible to distinguish if it was a man or woman, but I knew it was not a real person for it had a flimsy, opaque quality and no visible features.

My recollection of Spittlefields came to the rescue. Without much confidence, but feeling the situation called for some kind of action, I whispered, "Who are you? What do you want?" There was no reply and the figure just melted away. I knew I had not been dreaming – I had not been to sleep! Whatever had happened was for real!

The next day when I reflected on the night's events, I wasn't really too upset, although I could not claim to be overjoyed either. I accepted that a house could be haunted, but everything at Spittlefields had been presented in such a natural way that I didn't feel threatened by my ghostly visitor. It was sure to be an isolated event, at least I hoped so, as I had no wish for such experiences. However, my hopes were soon dashed and I became disturbed when visitations reoccurred on a regular basis. Sometimes two or three nights in a row I heard footsteps on the stairs and sensed the door opening after which the presence would go down the side of the bed and stand at the bottom looking at me. I somehow came to the conclusion that my unwelcome visitor was a man and there were times when I would speak and ask why he had come, or bless him and ask him to go away. At other times it was all too much and I shrank down in the big double bed, keeping my head firmly under the bedclothes until I instinctively knew he had left.

The climax came one night when I heard footsteps on the stairs and waited for him to enter in his usual way. Instead, the door was forcibly flung open and I felt a cold draught as the bedclothes were thrown back behind me and then, incredibly, the bed sank under the weight of someone getting in beside me. There was no sound or word. Could this really be happening? A cold tension gripped me and I was absolutely terrified! My first thought was that the house had been broken into and this was an intruder or burglar. My second thought was that a well aimed knee would be my best defence. So I hurled myself round – but there was not anyone there!

I had had enough! I decided then and there that I needed to confide in someone, and in spite of, or perhaps because of, his practical but kindly manner, I decided to talk to my father-in-law about it. It was difficult to gauge what his reaction might be. My mind went over and over what had happened and I pondered how I was going to tell him something so outlandish. It would be difficult to convince him that such events had taken place and it was practical to expect him to say that it wasn't possible. Afterwards I would have to leave. Having prepared and steeled myself for the ordeal, it was with almost disbelief that I heard him apologising for not letting me know that his wife's father, who had died some years earlier, still roamed the house and that she had seen him on several occasions. He had not wanted to alarm me, and out of consideration for my feelings and peace of mind had not told me of previous disturbances. Neither had he told me that I was sleeping in the old man's bed!

At his suggestion I confided in Rita and Norma who, knowing me to be practical and level headed in business, did not question the veracity of the matter and accepted the situation in true friendship. The outcome was that all three joined forces to ensure that in future I did not sleep in the house alone. And strangely, whilst they were there I was not aware of any further disturbances. It was as though the old man had made his point – I was trespassing in his bed and he wanted me to know it. Or, more likely, he wanted me out of it.

17

The sequel occurred some time later when my sister Joan and her husband came to visit for a few days whilst he was being demobilised from the army at a nearby camp. The day after they arrived was his big day and being an over conscientious hostess, I got up and cooked him breakfast. It was about 6.30 on a cold November morning when he left the house, far too early to start the day, so pouring myself a cup of tea I returned to the bed settee in the sitting room where I had spent the night.

At about 8.30 I made more tea and took a cup upstairs to my bedroom where Joan and her husband had slept. She opened her eyes and thanking me for the tea, laughed mischievously.

"I fooled you", she said.

"Did you? How?"

"When you came in earlier. I kept my eyes closed."

"What do you mean ..... when I came in earlier?"

"Well, you know. You came in softly and walked to the bottom of the bed, but I kept my eyes closed. I didn't want to get up so early."

Shortly afterwards my father-in-law and his wife moved back into the house and then Ron was demobilised, marking the beginning of a new and eventful life.

CHAPTER 3 – ENTER PETER

By the mid-1950's we were happily settled in a small, prosperous town set in the beautiful countryside of the south Midlands. We now had a young daughter and to supplement our income I had started a small business operating from home. Ron meanwhile, was studying and working hard in design engineering to try and make up for almost seven years he had lost to the army. And there was a lot of catching up to do. In common with many other young men, he had returned from the forces to find he was regarded as little more than a junior and was striving to prove his worth.

From time to time thoughts of my psychic experiences would come to mind, but always with a sense of isolation as I knew of no-one with a similar interest. It was maddening that Ron was so sceptical. He could not reconcile the ghostly visitations at his father's house with our own survival after death and ridiculed my ideas and beliefs. However, he always asserted that he was not afraid of death. As young lad he had had the unusual experience of hearing a doctor pronounce him dead whilst acutely ill in hospital with pneumonia. It was a vivid memory that stayed with him all his life and to which he often referred, saying, "There is nothing to fear. Dying is nothing more than sliding into a deep sleep."

It is not uncommon to find a reluctance among men, to acknowledge the existence of psychic phenomena or a spirit world, unless certain criteria can be met. Some need it to be explained in terms of the five physical senses or demonstrated repeatedly under laboratory conditions. Others require it to conform to their understanding of logic. At the root of this reluctance is often the fear of being thought foolish or gullible. I have found however, that when a man accepts that there is a spirit world he is usually steadfast in his belief as he will have arrived at his conclusions by means which will have satisfied his personal reasoning. On the whole women, being more intuitive, find it easier to accept the possibility of an afterlife and a spirit world, and are likely to want to know more.

It is unfortunate that in our culture, preconditioning by religious doctrine often creates a barrier that prevents both sexes from investigating the reality of a spirit world that interpenetrates with our own. This is in spite of the fact that both the New and Old Testaments of the bible are full of psychic happenings, healing, and intervention by God into human affairs.

It seemed to be just an informal, casual meeting over a cup of tea when we met Peter and Carol at the home of a mutual friend, but it proved to be a significant doorway, one destined to change our lives. They were an extremely attractive couple. She was an exhibition ballroom dancer, tall, stately with her pale, blonde hair piled high on her head. She was lovely and very sociable, whilst he had wit, boyish good looks and impeccable manners which added to his charm. They were slightly younger than us, recently married and as we were all mad about dancing and partying, we came to see a lot of each other. We thought we knew them well, but one evening, relaxing in our sitting room, Peter announced that his parents were moving up from London and would be living near us in the town. And, out of the blue, he confided that they were a family of Spiritualists!

When he was only six years old an uncle had taken Peter along to a Spiritualist church meeting. The impact of the people he met and what he heard and saw at the meeting, instilled in him an unusual curiosity for one so young. He badgered his parents to allow him to attend a lyceum – the Spiritualist church's equivalent to a C. of E. Sunday school, and he progressed from there to being a church member. In his early twenties he wondered whether he had been blinkered by having such an early introduction to this particular philosophy and ceased to go to church. A little later his business career began to take him all over the world including the Far East, Nepal, India and the Middle East, America and Africa. During these journeys he met and spoke with people of other religious persuasions and his beliefs turned a full circle and brought him back to the firm conviction that "Spiritualism is the most inclusive of religions".

A newspaper article written many years later when he became a town councillor quoted him as saying, "After I had met many different religious people I began to realise that the basic universal law at the root of all religions was eternity, spirituality and the fact that man progresses according to how he lives his lives." He went on to say that Spiritualists believe in one universal God and one universal set of natural and spiritual laws that govern all creation in whatever dimension it may be.

"Whereas other religions say you will believe this because I say so, or this book says so," he said, "this has not happened in Spiritualism. We say instead that you will experience this for yourself. Spiritualists will give guide lines, but at the end of the day, only your own experience will convince you whether there is a God and an afterlife or not."

He added the warning that seances and Ouija boards have no place in modern Spiritualism without proper supervision "It could be very dangerous to someone highly sensitive," he said. "Like a novice flying an aeroplane without supervision."

By the time we met he had already visited the Far East and Nepal and had been impressed by the people he had met. He had not the slightest doubt that what we call death is but the gateway to a new form of existence on a higher plane of life.

He had no hesitation in declaring, "As far as my consciousness is concerned, it is perfectly natural to communicate with people from the spirit world." Carol was tolerant but not at all convinced and both she and Ron soon tired of listening to our discussions which often went on quite late, until the night Ron went out of the room and came back in his pyjamas!

To me Peter was like a breath of fresh air. Not only was he sympathetic to my psychic experiences, but he answered many of the questions generated by events at Spittlefields and at my father-in-law's house. My talks with him confirmed my belief that we have existed before and will continue to exist after so-called death. This lifetime being only a very small part of eternity that can be likened to a room with a door at either end through which we must pass.

Peter came into our lives at exactly the right time. Not that I had been entirely idle up to meeting him as I wanted to know how, as a child, I had been able to see into the future. And did it happen to everyone, and if not, why me? My search had led me to the theory that Time is the fourth dimension of infinitive space. In this concept Time may be visualised as being laid out like a road. A road we are required to travel and where we are destined to meet certain experiences. With my limited education I did not find it an easy theory to follow, but it propounded a degree of fatalism that, at the time, had a certain appeal.

It suggested that if certain events are already in existence in an unknown (fourth) dimension of Time, then there is probably a natural explanation of how events may be seen ahead of our normal time scale. This brush with fatalism became complicated when through discussions with Peter, I came to recognise the importance of the Spiritualist principle of Personal Responsibility for all our thoughts and actions. If one accepts the Fourth Dimension and the theory of Predestination where certain events are preordained, how can this be equated with Personal Responsibility? And where does Precognition fit in? Doubtless there are others who could put forward a deeper explanation. But my understanding in simplistic terms, is that there is a Divine Plan for the world and within that plan is a pathway for each individual soul. No pathway is in isolation, but interacts with all others along the way. Along each plan and pathway there are certain experiences we are destined to meet, but there will always be choices and the opportunity to exercise personal or collective free will.

Perhaps this may be illustrated by visualising several interacting circumstances, which being in motion, are following their prescribed courses. If there are no deviations it should be possible to give an educated guess as to the outcome, or even an accurate forecast. It is possible that the spirit realms, being in a different dimension not subject to the limitations of our earthly time scale, have a wider overall view of our pathway and are able to correctly forecast events which lie in the future.

The situation may be similar to a traffic controller in a police helicopter who has an overall view of a motorway. He can see traffic congestion building up ahead and is able to direct traffic so that they may take avoiding action. Likewise he may see that if the pattern of certain erratic or dangerous driving is sustained, an accident is certain to occur and he may be able to pinpoint the exact place it will happen. Within these and similar circumstances drivers have personal responsibility and choice of action. They may heed police advice and leave the motorway to avoid congestion, or take warning and change their mode of driving, or, conceivably, they may disregard advice and warnings and choose to continue as before with predictable results.

This hypothesis has given me some measure of understanding although it must be appreciated that I am using my limited human intelligence and applying reason with my finite mind. Although it is pleasing to arrive at an explanation that satisfies the intellect, it is often the intellect itself which forms a barrier to greater understanding. Matters of the spirit are more likely to be understood intuitively through a deeper consciousness than by rational thinking and application of human standards.

From time to time I have had experiences of precognition during sleep state that have fallen into three categories. A few have been similar to the preview of the extermination camp; events that are far into the future and appear to serve me no purpose. Among those was the funeral of Gamal Abdul Nasser the Egyptian President who was assassinated in 1970, and again the newsreels were identical to my "dream". Another which took years to come to fruition involved hundreds of pilgrims to Mecca who were trapped in a fire disaster. This last vision was foretold to our group at the time I saw it, but as I say, doesn't appear to have served any purpose.

Other instances of precognition have drawn me to the conclusion that the veil is drawn aside when it will be helpful to me, such as the time when in a "dream" I saw my parents and other members of my family standing round a freshly dug grave. They were not sad, in fact I noted they were relaxed and smiling. I peered down into the grave which was lined with artificial grass, and found it empty! The tricky part is of course, the interpretation! My conclusion was that someone in the family was going to be very ill but that it would not be fatal. The one person missing from the graveside was my sister Joan and I thought that if I told her that someone was going to be ill but that it would not be fatal, it would be helpful to her if she were to be the victim. I also told my parents to be prepared for a family illness. In the event, within a month, my father had a heart attack, the first of several. It was a significant event in our parents' lives as it marked the beginning of twelve years as a semi-invalid for dad. My vision was a blessing for the family, because although the illness could not be averted, they were spared a great deal of worry and anxiety in the knowledge that he was going to pull through that first attack.

The third category of precognition comes into play when I am trying to help others through healing or counselling. Often a glimpse into the future proves valuable to the recipient, but equally useful is a look into the past to find the underlying cause of an existing health problem. It seems that past events along our pathway are not obscured, but remain visible to those with the sensitivity to see.

Peter and I often regretted the fact that there were no other people around with similar interests to our own, except of course his parents Harry and Phyllis who had helped to run churches in London and Devon. We were quite unaware that for several years a small group had been holding weekly Spiritualist meetings in a house on the far side of town. It therefore came out of the blue to see an advertisement for the proposed formation of a Spiritualist church. We could not begin to speculate who might be behind it, but were naturally interested and very curious to know more. Although I could not have persuaded Ron to attend the meeting, our discussions must have had some affect for he volunteered to come with Peter, Carol and me. Luckily I had secretly bought him a ticket!

By this time I had put to good use my experience of office systems, recruitment and personnel and had opened offices in a relevant service industry. I was now well known in town and not knowing who the organisers were it seemed wise that we should not sit as a group, but split up so as not to hint at our relationships.

The inaugural meeting had attracted a large number of people and when we arrived the hall was getting full. We had not known what to expect and were pleasantly surprised to find that the President of the Spiritualists National Union was to give the address. Gordon Higginson, a natural psychic from childhood, had been rigorously trained to be a platform demonstrator by his mother, herself a medium. Much to his chagrin she barred him from appearing in churches and demonstrating in public until he had developed his gifts to an outstanding level of competence. It is to her credit that she ensured that he would not be content with demonstrating anything less that than the highest possible spiritual guidance. This had meant long patient years of meditation and study, until he achieved close communication with his guides and was confident that the messages and information he relayed would be reliable and accurate. He was a man of exceptional psychic ability and the channel for detailed, evidential messages that were intimate and meaningful to recipients. He often amazed audiences by including in his messages full identification with surnames, place names and numbers.

The meeting that evening heard of his early beginnings, and he then went on to explain that in 1958 modern Spiritualism had become recognised as a religion with the same legal standing as any other religion. Their Ministers are able to conduct marriages, funerals and naming ceremonies etc. Gordon explained that members are asked to recognise Seven Principles on which the philosophy of Spiritualism is based, and listed them as The Fatherhood of God, The Brotherhood of Man, The Communion of Spirits and the Ministry of Angels, The Continuous Existence of the Human Soul, Personal Responsibility, Compensation and Retribution Hereafter for all the good and evil deeds done on earth, and finally, Eternal Progress open to every human soul.

He told his rapt audience that given the right conditions, Spiritualism seeks to prove what all other religions preach – continuation of life after death. He explained that when we die we shed our earthly outer body and release our spirit into a new dimension – a new plane of existence that operates on finer vibrations than those of the earth plane. What we call death is but a natural rebirth and how we conduct our lives here will determine our spiritual status in the afterlife.

So many people are instinctively aware that there is more to life than appears on the surface. Life should mean more than working, taking holidays and leading a purely materialistic life. He asserted that awareness of an afterlife, proven through communication with those who have passed on, could change the lives of those present and give them a spiritual purpose for living. He urged his audience not to accept his word, but investigate for themselves with an open mind, and he had no doubt that their lives would be happier and more content. Most impressive stuff!

I had been surprised to see Lillian, a friend who owned a manufacturing company, taking an active role among the organisers of the meeting, as I had no idea that she was interested in such matters. But it was she who telephoned me the following morning to ask whom I thought might be President of the new church and I had no hesitation in recommending Peter. He readily agreed, and with Harry as Secretary we quickly got off the ground by hiring a room in a public building for weekly meetings.

This occurred in the early sixties when there were many mature and dedicated mediums serving churches in the south Midlands. They had been operating since before the church had gained statutory respectability and all were eager to offer guidance and help. Additionally, they freely gave their time and demonstrated their excellent mediumship. It was apparent from the outset that they were drawn to Ron, as week after week various demonstrators singled him out as a potential powerful healer. They would see him surrounded by an aura of the deepest, clearest blue which signifies healing energy, and repeatedly urged him to allow himself to be used as a channel for Spiritual healing. But being naturally shy and reticent, he was most reluctant to put it to the test, and chose to ignore the door that was being held open for him.

As a new church it was obviously desirable to establish a core of people at least as informed and developed as Peter and his parents. To this end a development circle was formed under the guidance of a long estab-lished and experienced medium from another church. It was important to begin in this way because any group sitting together for the purpose of com-municating with the spirit world should ensure that they are under the direc-tion of an experienced medium who has the help and protection of her own (known) highly evolved guides and helpers. To do otherwise would be simi-lar to opening the front and back doors of ones home and allowing any stranger to enter.

When people pass into the next world they are not transformed into superior beings, but take with them their intelligence and spiritual understanding which will include their prejudices and attitudes. Those who demonstrated anti-social behaviour in their earthly lifetime, will continue in the same frame of mind. Others, because of the nature of their passing, may be consumed with hatred against their fellow men and seek revenge by cre-ating mischief or influencing others to commit evil. They may attach to a particular person and those playing with Ouija boards for fun, or experi-menting by sitting in an unprotected circle are easy targets.

When we embarked on our circle work we didn't know our own guides and placed ourselves under the guardianship of the experienced medium's guides, in good faith that no undesirable entity would be allowed to infringe our meetings. Some call these guides "door-keepers" as their function is to protect and not allow unwelcome spirits to intrude.

Peter and Carol kindly let us meet once a week at their house and we began to build up the right conditions for our own personal guides to make themselves known to us. It was a slow process of visualisation and interpretation, and gradually most of us realised that we were clairvoyant. Only one sitter proved to be clairaudient, although from time to time others heard the odd word or phrase from spirit. We were a happy group, united by common purpose. We all wished to work towards a successful, established church and aspired to form a healing clinic. It was this unified motivation which made us so compatible and we made steady progress including Ron whose meditation was deep but otherwise unremarkable.

The psychic gifts that enable a medium to become a channel by which messages can be conveyed from the spirit world, can be categorised as clairvoyance (clear seeing), clairaudience (clear hearing) and clairsen-tience (mental impression). These three gifts provide the most satisfactory channels by which accurate evidence may be obtained. Healing is a separate channel working on a different vibration and as will be seen, may work in conjunction with any or all of the other three. However, possession of these gifts is without value unless the medium, or channeller, can correctly inter-pret that which spirit is trying to transmit. Hence the years of practice that are often required to gain competency and reliability.

After sitting in a circle and learning to relax and meditate, it is often possible to assist psychic development by practising automatic writing or psychometry. But this was unknown to me until one evening after a church service when I was thanking the visiting medium for her excellent service. She clasped my hand in both of hers and asked. "Do you do psychometry?"

"No" I vaguely replied, not really understanding what she meant.

She smiled, "My dear, you will. Before my next visit. You will see."

I had no idea what I was expected to do until I read that it is possible to hold an article, say a piece of jewellery, and obtain impressions of the person who has previously handled or worn it. Additionally, places and events connected with the person's past may be seen by the handler's inward clairvoyant eye. It is an ancient belief that people leave their imprint on objects they have handled and in their surroundings. Material objects absorb the essence of their owners and often the circumstances and surroundings in which they existed, although it is not known how long these impressions last. Some ancient buildings seem to harbour within their walls atmospheric conditions many decades or centuries after particularly disagreeable events. Sensitive people may find they are unable to wear secondhand jewellery that in the past has absorbed sad events, or have in their homes pieces of antique pottery or metal which appear to communicate sadness or ill-ease. These moods could transfer to the new owner and it follows that it is unwise for persons of a nervous disposition to attempt psychometry. However, this skill can be useful for developing psychic ability.

The visiting medium's prophecy seemed a tall order, but never one to avoid a challenge, I was soon wearing the patience of friends by taking ages to produce even the smallest shred of evidence. I find the best material to use is metal and it is essential to me that the article should have been owned by only one person. When more than one person has owned say, a ring or watch, results can be confusing. It took a great deal of practice before I was able to produce good clairvoyant pictures in full colour which were meaningful to the sitter. It is particularly satisfying to both parties when I have not met the sitter before, or know very little about him or her.

There are many examples of highly developed psychometric mediums who are consulted by the police in cases of missing persons and these are well documented. But I was only at the experimental stage when a young junior typist in my office enquired if I thought I could get results from an earring. She was a quiet, reserved girl who had been with us only a short time but she obviously had been chatting with other members of staff, all of whom knew of my weird interest in the paranormal. I agreed to see her in a lunch break and we settled down in two chairs facing each other. Holding the earring in my closed fist, I got an immediate, clear picture of a dark, good looking young woman in a grey silk dress that had a cross-over bodice. She wore earrings. She looked fully at me and smiled and as she did so I felt a warm wave of love and affection sweep over me which I knew was for my sitter. She was standing on a footpath in front of a grey brick house that had a long, narrow front garden and wooden gate. On the opposite side of the path ran a stream or ditch. As I related this to my sitter, a spinning car wheel came into view. Then I saw that it was attached to a car that was lying upside down. The car was impacted against a tall pole. I could not move my focus from the wheel which continued to spin and block out further images. I cut the "reading" at that point – it had taken only a few minutes.

It was gratifying to have immediate confirmation of the details of the house, path and ditch, also the description of my sitter's mother to whom the earring belonged and who was central to the reading. It was an extremely emotional experience for both of us, as I had not known that her mother had died and my heart went out to her.

Afterwards I was horrified to learn that her father had deliberately rammed their car into a telegraph pole during an argument. Although he had wished for them all to die, he and his young daughter survived. He had only recently come out of prison after serving a sentence for manslaughter and his daughter, now eighteen, was desperately unhappy to be sharing a house with him. She came into the office the next day with a photograph of her mother in the same silk dress with the cross-over bodice, standing in front of the gate of the brick house.

One could question whether the message had been facilitated by psychometry or telepathy as my sitter was naturally emotional and anxious to know if her mother could possibly have survived. I have no doubt that her emotional state helped to achieve results. I also know from the love that flowed over and through me, that it was a true spirit communication. Since then I have not questioned the source of my inspiration but have been content to convey evidential proof of survival whenever I could.

The happy consequence of the sitting was that Harry and Phyllis, Peter's parents, took her into their home. Unfortunately, and quite unforeseen, this triggered threats and harassment by her father until police protection became necessary. Throughout this episode the love and support she received from her new friends was unconditional. We all believed she had been guided to my office at a time when she was in a potentially dangerous situation and in need of friends, spiritual upliftment and reassurance. Naturally she had been impressed by the reading and wanted to understand what had happened to her mother. To this end we invited her to become part of our meditation and discussion group. This gave her the opportunity of learning about continuation of life beyond death, and she came to understand that although human personality and intelligence survive death, any injury, disfigurement, pain or illness cease to exist with the death of the physical body. Where love has been strong the bonds of love cannot be broken – not even by death. Where our dear ones wish to help us along our way, they may at times be closer to us after their transition than they were before. But the choice is theirs – we cannot call them back. It is not desirable or right for us to cling to someone who has passed through the gateway to the other side of life, or mourn them to the extent that they are distressed for us, and held back and prevented from progressing along their natural pathway.

When giving sittings I find it practical and satisfying to insist that sitters respond only with "Yes" or "No" and do not volunteer information. To be given information not only disrupts concentration but might influence my interpretation of what is being channelled. More importantly, it would not be evidential to sitters if they were allowed to volunteer information. In fact the best evidence is to be able to supply facts that are unknown to the sitter and require to be checked through a relative, or by some other means. As any message is only as good as the channeller's interpretation, it is important the medium mentally queries with the guide anything that is unclear before passing it on to the sitter. The aim of any sitting should be to provide evidential proof of survival and it follows that asking the sitter questions, or giving vague descriptions and generalisations do not achieve this goal.

CHAPTER 5 – HEALING ENERGY

Some time after the commencement of the Development Circle, Ron and I decided the time had come when we could no longer put off having our house decorated, and set about making the necessary arrangements. It was a big effort to move furniture so that a decorator could work undisturbed in the bedrooms. Unfortunately he proved to be disastrously inefficient and after the ceiling paper fell down and draped itself over the wardrobes, it was time for emergency measures. Which was how we came to be sleeping on a mattress on the sitting room floor! When I awoke the following morning, I was absolutely stiff and could not turn or lift myself. This was not unusual as it had been a recurring problem since our daughter had been born some eighteen years earlier. In a bed I could use the frame as leverage, but here I was at floor level and helpless. Ron, of course, was used to being asked to help and when I told him I could not move he did not reply but slid his arm round my waist and we lay quietly without a word. After a few moments he said he would go and make a cup of tea. I was still lying on my side facing the fireplace, when I had the sudden sensation of water being thrown at me at waist level. I could have sworn there were waves of water pulsating down my lower body and legs and I shot upright with no effort at all! As I called out, Ron hurried in from the kitchen and I incredulously told him what had occurred.

I looked at him and asked. "Did you try to heal me?"

Self-consciously he smiled and reluctantly admitted that yes, he had tried, he had prayed and asked for proof that he could be a healer.

It was then, without thought, I was inspired to say "Well, you have had your proof. You can heal, but you will never find it so easy again."

It was a peculiar off-the-cuff remark but I intuitively knew there was much hard work to do and a long way to go. Our daughter is now in her fifties and, blessedly, I have never once had a repetition of the condition. In fact, my back is remarkably strong.

This experience whilst wonderfully beneficial to me, was I am sure, intended to prove to Ron that he could be a channel for healing. He would never have taken the first step without it. A little later when a healing clinic was formed under the guidance of an experienced healer and we set about getting our qualifications from the Guild of Spiritualist Healers, he and I happily formed one of the teams. It was then that the power and truth of Spiritual healing began to manifest itself and the clinic's four teams were able to bring about wonderful relief and cures. Most were routine and have paled into insignificance over the years, although they were nonetheless effective at the time and on clinic evenings there was always a queue waiting for attention. Others stand out vividly in my memory.

I well recall one young man in his teens who came to the clinic and joined those who not only filled the reception room but overflowed onto the stairs. It was some considerable time before his turn came, and he limped into our room saying he had injured his leg and was in a lot of pain. We asked him to sit on a chair and Ron administered to his back whilst I sat on a stool in front of him, first holding his hands, and then paying attention to his leg. The patient was then asked to stand up and Ron worked on his leg whilst he was standing. Afterwards I asked the young man to walk to the far corner of the room. He strode there!

When I smiled and said "There. How is that then?" He tersely replied "Well, that's what I came for, isn't it?"

Hardly gracious, but he had indeed got what he came for. The following week a patient marvelled that she had seen him running to the bus station after his healing session.

Such cases of faith are in contrast to those patients, of which there were far too many, who turned up at the clinic every week, and when asked how they were, responded, "Well, I have had a good week, until this morning when it (sic) started aching again." Psychologically, they were ready for their weekly dose of 'asprin'. One may be forgiven for thinking that with a little more belief and faith they might have overcome the weekly cycle. But we would not refuse help to anyone who asked for it, neither would we accept personal payment although it was often offered. A church collection box was on display in the reception, but our services were free to all who came.

Hannah, a lady in her 60's who lived in a nearby market town was recommended to the clinic and brought to us by her son. She was heavily built and severely arthritic, and it took much leverage and several pairs of kind hands to get her up the stairs and into our room. It was obvious she was experiencing a great deal of pain and a blessing that she obtained some relief on her first visit. Encouraged she came to us regularly and eventually after many weeks, she was able to discard one of her walking sticks. It took several months before she could walk freely and after many years of suffering was able to resume a normal life, walking to the nearby shops and doing her own housework.

At this time Ron and I had two helpers who sat in the room with us. One was Peter's mother Phyllis an experienced healer herself, and the other Jane, was one of the nicest, kindest and most spiritual people one could wish to meet. Her manner towards everyone she met radiated love and goodness. The power from these two helpers contributed in no small

31

amount to our success but the main source of healing energy emanated from the spirit doctors who worked through Ron. The force was tangible. We could all feel the heat that flowed through him and there were times when healers and patient would be bathed in perspiration.

There were two remarkable occasions when healers and patient saw healing energy radiating like porcupine quills from his palms. He was working with his hands about eight centimetres from Hannah's ankle and the "quills" bridged the gap. The thin shafts of light were clear, brilliant lilac - a sight never forgotten by those present, except of course Ron who was unaware of the phenomena. Both occasions reinforced our understanding that we were instruments of a benign and natural force, although not pretending to understand the energies involved.

During healing Ron would be overshadowed by his guide, a doctor. Not only would his facial features alter and his voice change, but his posture would become that of a bent old man. The change was so dramatic that even those who were not psychic were able to identify the guide's presence before he spoke. This dear mentor made himself known to us from the earliest days of the clinic and remained with us through all our activities. He would be with us the instant we wished to start healing, usually before the patient was seated – never once was there delay or reason for disappointment. His love and guidance were palpable and we have always had great respect for him and felt secure in his hands. It is known that "like" on the earth plane attracts "like" from the spirit world, and his guide is so similar to Ron that it is uncanny. When in the early days I made the mistake of asking his name, I was politely brushed aside.
His reply was, "Who I am does not matter. It is the work that counts."

It was evident he delighted in working through Ron who was also modest and unassuming. I believe that it was this lack of ego, this humility, that helped provide an open channel through which the healing energies could freely flow.

A special and personal instance of healing was when Ron's brother Bob, paid a visit to our home. It was a rare event as they were not a close family, Ron's two elder brothers having left home in their teens to take up employment in other parts of the country. Consequently, neither he nor his wife Elsie knew anything of our interest in the esoteric. Bob was certainly not religious in the traditional sense, but I don't think he was agnostic or irreligious either. During the afternoon, somehow, and one never knows how these things start, conversation veered away from the norm and we were telling them of the healing clinic. A highly qualified engineer used to thinking in terms of black and white, Bob thought it too nebulous and high flown for his taste. We couldn't have expected him to be other than sceptical and derisive and it was evident he thought his youngest brother had taken leave of his senses, or was under the power of some machinations of mine! Ron, meanwhile, was silently asking his guide to get him "out of this mess" and if it were possible, to provide his brother with some proof.

Suddenly Bob exclaimed, "What's going on here? What are you doing to me?" He wrenched off his shoes and stood up. As he hobbled across the carpet we could see that without specially made shoes he could only walk on the outside of his feet. He told us that the last items of clothing he took off at night before getting into bed were his shoes, as he could not bear the pain of standing up without them. This was news to us. However, he accepted that magically he had been able to walk across our room without shoes and without pain, and acknowledged that something peculiar had happened. He then asked us to give him healing, the effect of which was very good and sustained for several months. It would have been remarkable if one session had been enough, and we would have liked to have seen him regularly. But it was not to be as he lived in the south of England, several hours journey away.

That visit and the healing, forged a new relationship between the two brothers, and for several years we joined up to go abroad for our holidays. It was then that Bob welcomed a healing session before we went out each evening, with excellent results. It was during these holidays that Bob took opportunities, when he and Ron were alone, to enquire into our beliefs, and I believe Ron was able to talk to him in some depth.

In earlier years before we had started holidaying together, Bob had suffered a cancerous growth in his neck and had blessedly recovered after radiation treatment. But when, in his seventies, he had a severe heart attack and had to be resuscitated, he knew his quality of life would never be the same. He hated the thought of living life as an invalid and privately told his son-in-law that he had no wish to recover on those terms. Within a couple of days he died quietly and contentedly. How much his courage can be attributed to Ron's influence may only be surmised, but undoubtedly, his attitude towards life and death had undergone a profound change.

In the clinic we worked as separate teams and patients would invariably see the same healer each time. However, sometimes a quality would be lacking, perhaps an incompatibility at some level, and the healing would not be effective. Another team would then be asked to take the patient over and this often had better results. But there are no guarantees in healing, all is carried out by the Grace of God, and as a healer, all one asks is that patients approach the healing session with an open mind, and do not put up an invisible but tangible barrier of scepticism.

Although not connected with the clinic there was the memorable occasion when Ron and I were on holiday in Looe. We had rented a cottage on the sea front with two friends, both healers in a church some distance from our own. The holiday had passed happily, Ron drawing while I painted and our friends explored the area. Two weeks passed very quickly and the final Saturday morning had arrived with the two cars packed, ready at the door for the journeys home. Everything was clean and tidy but I did a last minute fussing around during which I tried to straighten an armchair. Not realising it was a heavy, iron framed bed-settee I had raised it only two or three inches before it slipped through my fingers onto the big toe of my foot. The nail split from top to bottom. I quickly asked for a bowl of hot water and rejecting all suggestion of getting a doctor, asked one of the men to dash to the main street and get bandages. By the time it had been bathed half the nail was standing up like a sail and it took firm bandaging to press it down. All this time the toe felt very hot and it was agreed I had been badly shaken and should go and lie down.

I went into the first bedroom I came to. It was not one we had used and finding a double bunk for children, I rolled onto the bottom bed. As I lay on my side I was feeling very sorry for myself and at the same time guilty for putting everyone to so much trouble. Suddenly I became aware of an old man with white hair and exceptionally rosy cheeks sitting in the far corner diagonal to the bed. The light around him was very bright. He smiled and held out his arms which stretched across the room until his hands cupped around my foot without actually touching it. He radiated power and love. I felt a wave of contentment and said "Thank you. God bless you," and promptly fell fast asleep! I have no doubt that at about the same time Ron and the other two healers would have been giving me absent healing.

When I awoke some three hours later it was to find that the owners of the cottage had phoned to say that they would not be using the property that weekend and we could stay an extra two days. The cars had already been off loaded! That afternoon I walked a short distance with the others to local gardens and climbed steep steps to a seat overlooking the beach and the sea. Incredibly I experienced no pain, neither that afternoon nor any at time in the future, although the nail was bandaged or plastered until it became whole six months later.

That dear healer has helped at other times when I have been able to bring relief to others who have injured hands or feet. Personally, I think I am more careless than most as I have since injured my toes and fingers on several occasions. Particularly nasty was when I was helping to build a rockery in our garden, and dropped a boulder on the same big toe! Recently when I lacked concentration, I caught two fingers in a small electric whisk although on that occasion I had to receive first aid at the local hospital. At the first opportunity I have quietly pictured this dear old man with his rosy cheeks, sat in a brightly lit part of a room, and asked for his help. He has never let me down, and although shaken, I have never experienced pain from my injuries which have taken the normal time, and yards of plaster, to heal.

Healing is a natural power and freely available. If someone in discomfort or pain believes in the benevolence and power of the spirit world and asks for healing for himself, in addition to medical treatment he might be receiving, it is possible that he may find he can draw to himself the Divine universal healing energy. This is not to be confused with positive thought which can be applied to cheering ourselves up, or looking at the compensations in life. It is everything to do with recognising that healing is a natural energy emanating from God the source of all energies. To pray to God and ask for His help creates the right conditions for healing energy to manifest.

Spiritual healers work in harmony with doctors in the spirit world who have learned to channel the natural healing energy to them, and through them to their patients. The energy is directed to the spiritual aspect of the patient which in turn, reacts on the physical body. It is therefore essential that patient and healer are in sympathy with each other, and channels are open to allow the energy to flow. As with the medical profession, it isn't possible to always obtain a cure, but with this type of healing, where there is no resistance, it is always possible to obtain a measure of relief without the use of drugs. And whilst mentioning drugs, it is not desirable that they be reduced or withdrawn without the agreement or direction of a medical practitioner.

Spiritual healing is the utilisation of a natural energy by a healer who doesn't heal, but is merely a channel for the manifestation to take place. The ability to do so is one of the Gifts of the Spirit, but it is desirable for healers to undertake training and work within a code of conduct that conforms to the codes of practices laid down by the medical profession, dentists, midwives and veterinary surgeons. This protects both healer and patient from malpractice. In this context, the approach to Spiritual healing is that it should always be regarded as a complementary therapy and not an alternative to orthodox medicine.

CHAPTER 6 – JOURNEY WITH A MONK

Our church premises proved to be a convenient venue and services were always well attended, but to widen our appeal, and bring our ideals to more people, I organised publicity meetings. The committee agreed that although we would have to pay heavier expenses for first class national and international mediums, it could be well worth while. I was aware that inviting the Press had its risks as it could potentially expose us to ridicule from a profession usually seeking to promote the sensational side of our "ism". However, because of the high standard of these mediums who could be relied upon to give evidence of survival, I decided to invite Donald, chief reporter on the local paper. I got to know him well, not only through these meetings, but also in the general way of business and was pleased that he gave us very fair write-ups, sometimes even enthusiastic. He was a tall, lean, untidy figure with a straggly beard and bright humorous eyes. An interesting man who had previously enquired into various forms of Extra Sensory Perception (E.S.P). and was adept at self hypnosis, although he knew little of our philosophy.

When, one afternoon, the receptionist 'phoned through to say that Donald was asking to see me, I said he should be shown to an interview room and found him seated on a settee with a young reporter next to him, notebook at the ready.

Apologetically Donald started, "I'm sorry to barge in like this in working hours, but I have a something that's turned up in a field, and I'm wondering if you can identify it for me? It's rather important."

"Well", I replied taken aback. "I'll look at it. But it's not convenient to do anything with it at the moment. And," glancing towards the young reporter, "I wouldn't wish my name to be published in association with anything psychic." My natural wish to protect my business interests was readily understood. Fishing in his pocket, Donald agreed. "Of course. I understand that. But please look at it. I can leave it with you, but it's rather urgent."

As he spoke he handed me a small piece of metal about three quarters of an inch high and the same in width. It was fashioned like a small crown and if I had been asked to guess what it was, I might have said, "A knob from an ancient pot or vase." It was difficult to say what the metal was, but it appeared to be lead which, over time, had become coated with a white substance. He went on, "Whatever the outcome, I can promise you that you will not be named or identified. I would just be grateful if you would do it." With that reassurance and knowing he could be trusted, I told him I would take it home and contact him in a day or two.

Even as I spoke I became aware of a figure standing in front of me, and followed on by saying, "But there is a monk in a long brown habit who has just come into the room!"

There was no choice but to go on, so I asked them to sit quietly and please, not to volunteer any information. Closing my eyes I began a clairvoyant journey which I recited as it occurred. I have the clearest recollection of following the monk into country surroundings and along the outside wall of a grey stone building. We rounded a corner and proceeded down the side of a longer wall until we came to a short flight of four or five stone steps that led down into a long rectangular room. The dimness was relieved by light from burning rushes that were held in conical shaped containers fixed at intervals along the wall. A scrubbed refractory table ran three quarters of the way down the centre of the room and had benches on either side. The table was set with wooden bowls.

The monk led me to the end of the room where a small altar table stood central against the wall. At that end the whole wall was covered by an intricate ornamental screen. It was beautifully crafted in a trellis design with leaves, tendrils and roses. The monk walked across to the right hand side of the screen and smilingly pointed to a rose the centre of which was missing. He had the "crown" in his hand and holding it on its side placed it exactly into the space at the heart of the rose. Still smiling at me he turned to leave and indicated by extending his hand that I should follow him outside. As I reached the top of the steps the familiar outline of distant hills met my view and I knew we were facing west. I was also shown orchards heavy with rosy apples and dotted with beehives and knew the monks produced mead and cider for the parent abbey.

The vision faded and I was back with the journalists. It had been so crystal clear that I immediately volunteered to sketch a plan of the building. Donald was on the point of telling me about the field where the metal had been found but I stopped him as I felt other artifacts might follow, as indeed they later did.

It was a couple of weeks later when the entire front page of the local newspaper was devoted to an account of finding a buried chapel that was doubtless related to a near-by abbey. Donald had taken a water diviner from a local utility company to the site, but had not shown him my plan. The article related that by using his skill as a dowser, the man had found and traced the buried foundations of a building. The plan he drew exactly co-ordinated with my own. His drawing, published in the centre of the page, showed a gap where I had found steps. In all other respects our drawings were identical. The dimensional proportions and the building's relation to the western hills were confirmed. Donald had kept his word and I was only referred to as "a local medium" which was amusing for I certainly did not think of myself in those terms. But it was an interesting exercise that did me and the church no harm at all.

Some time later there was an archaeological dig when more pieces of the screen were unearthed. There were also some small pieces of bone that I identified as being part of a magnificent chestnut horse. When I described the cottage near his stable and an adjacent oak, I was told these still existed. But I declined to go to the site being satisfied that I had played my part in helping Donald with his enquiries and at the same time, had done something to recompense him for his objective reporting of our meetings.

This incident was important to me as it expanded my understanding of a fourth dimension of time. It placed us in the middle of a road from where it is possible to travel not only forward but also backward. Not just recent events could be seen, but events in the past were evidently still clear. That it is demonstrably possible to see both the future and the past, suggests certain events that affect not only individuals but the world in general, already exist in another dimension not understood by our limited intelligence. Shakespeare may have had this in mind when he wrote that the world is a stage and men and women merely players. But actors are tied to a script, whilst in the real world, we have choice and freewill within the parameters allowed us, and are responsible for our own actions.

In spite of my small success with psychometric readings, there was no temptation to give demonstrations on church platforms. By nature I aspired to perfection, and did not consider myself competent for such work. I certainly did not want to join the ranks of underdeveloped mediums who give vague messages full of generalisations to pad out the time allotted to them. Whilst to some extent entertaining, and sometimes amusing, the ego of such mediums may be more easily satisfied than the congregation. Being strong on organisation, it suited me to arrange social events, produce a regular church magazine and run a bookstall. We had an enthusiastic team and raised funds by jumble sales, garden parties, suppers and outings. All helped towards building a successful and living church.

At the same time I had many business interests – there were not enough hours in a day. They were blessed times when I was at peak physical energy and privileged to feel very close to those in the spirit world who were guiding me. It was then that I had an inkling of the need for balance between the material and the spiritual in our daily lives, but there were so many demands on my time that it seemed an impossibility.

The need for balance had been prompted to a large extent by reading of the need for positive thought and right thinking. I became an avid reader of books on the nature of man and those that attempted to understand the Divine Power whom we call God. I was particularly attracted to a writer who propounded a positive belief in the existence of a Divine order and a Divine pattern in all things. He encouraged readers to believe that the Divine Love of God is manifest in all things, and that even when events seem to be conspiring against us, the hand of God is guiding us towards an unseen and unknown betterment.

Initially it was difficult to believe that we are always in the right place at the right time as my domestic situation was difficult due to continual interference from my mother-in-law and Ron's guilt at what he saw as his part in her unhappiness. But through study I found I could accept this difficult situation as being part of my spiritual development, knowing it to be transient and believing that what really matters is not the problem but how we deal with it.

Nothing can stop our spiritual growth and unfoldment, although we progress at our own pace and in our own time, according to our spiritual awareness and our desire to do so. It is part of the natural order that each soul will develop, expand and grow although it may take interminable time to make considerable progress. Spiritual growth is inevitable and it is in the nature of man that this be so.

It was around this time that I began to appreciate the need for conscious thought control and came to believe not only that we are what we have thought, but we will become what we now think. Our thoughts, singularly and collectively, are the breeding ground for so much suffering and disharmony that is often erroneously attributed to God. We ask why certain events are allowed to happen, overlooking the fact that they have been set in motion by mens' own thoughts and subsequent actions. Thoughts are the motivation for all we do, and fear may bring about the very things we fear. Unconstrained thoughts of criticism, envy and malice will create disharmony and division, and certainly generate unhappiness and ill-health in ourselves. Conversely, thinking positively and charitably draws people to us and we become the recipients of kindness, friendship and love.

Forgiveness, guilt and revenge had never entered my thinking. From childhood I had been taught that God was the ultimate arbiter and that everyone would be judged responsible for his own actions. I believed, and still do, that revenge is not mine to give. But my thoughts on personal responsibility had strengthened since I had found its inclusion in the principles of the church, together with the parallel concept that after our passing there would be compensation and retribution for our actions here on earth. It is up to each living soul to strive to live to his highest moral understanding and to cling to principles of absolute love, order, wholeness, harmony and infinite Goodness.

I came upon the statement that "Of ourselves we can do nothing, and without God we are nothing. We are, because God is." But I was not ready to take this on board or understand it. Being successful in all aspects of my material life through hard work, diligence and a will to succeed, albeit aggressively, I was naturally proud of my achievements and had confidence in myself and my own abilities. The statement seemed to undermine and diminish me as a person and it was only many years later that I came to understand its truth.

CHAPTER 7 – SPIRIT COMMUNICATION

Although we differed in our rate of development, the church circle members gradually came to identify their own Gifts of the Spirit and recognised that the bond that united us was the gift of healing. It was as though we had been brought together for that specific purpose.

We found we were open to communication with the spirit world through inspiration, intuition, clairvoyance, and later, as we progressed, through healing. Those in the world of spirit may desire to get in touch with us and can do so, if they are able. Their contact with us is always voluntary and we are unable to impinge on their world as they can on ours. We cannot call back the so-called dead. But if we are sensitive and have the right motives, we can facilitate contact with guides and guardian angels. Under their guidance and protection we can attune ourselves to become a medium or channel through which communication and healing energies may flow.

It has been pointed out earlier that it is not difficult for spirit entities to contact sitters especially when the latter are endeavouring to make contact purely for amusement. Toying with Ouija boards has no place in Spiritualism as it can be an attraction to mischievous or inferior spirits who are still attached to the earth plane. Spirits who were anti-social or mischievous in their lifetime, may seek to influence those still here, or take delight in playing tricks on those unaware of the dangers. Such communication might seem fun but the results could be deeply disturbing and harmful, and what is more, difficult to dispel. To sit alone or with others, for the sole purpose of trying to contact the spirit realms can be a dangerous exercise.

There are others who take a normal transition but do not recognise their state of survival. They may have led decent, ordinary lives but because of their ignorance remain nearer to the earth's physical vibrations than those of the next plane. Unfortunately, some who remain close to the earth stay attached to their old familiar surroundings and whilst not meaning any harm, may disturb those sensitive to their presence, as was the case in my father-in-law's house. People do not become saints when they pass into the next life, neither do they suddenly acquire wisdom and light. They are exactly the same as when they were here. They pass into the next world with the same intelligence and the same spiritual understanding, the same prejudices and the same principles. As has been said, and it bears repeating, to sit without the protection of an experienced medium and her known guides and guardian angels, is similar to opening the doors of one's home and inviting any stranger to enter.

There are no short cuts to the valuable years of training that are essential to establish knowledge of one's guides and helpers and develop clear intercommunication. A humbleness of heart is essential. Those who embark on this path to satisfy their ego may achieve success as clairvoyants or psychics but rarely achieve deep understanding of spiritual values. Indeed, they will often go through their lives absolving their own weaknesses and shortcomings as just "being human", not realising the spiritual growth that can be achieved in an earthly lifetime.

When establishing communication with the spirit world, it is our responsibility to provide conditions of sincere prayer, love and harmony. These are essential characteristics of a successful development circle, healing group or church. If negative qualities such as envy, back-biting, resentment, discontent, grandiosity or egotism are allowed to intrude, groups will never attain the harmony and tranquillity that our guides and. guardian angels require to do their best work. Further, if negative qualities exist, we may be opening ourselves to undesirable communication with those in the lower realms of the spirit world whose influence may be harmful to us.

By deep, sincere prayer in which we let it be known that we wish to contact only the highest sources of inspiration and wisdom, we can create the right conditions for uniting with the highest spiritual beings it is possible for us to contact. In a group where harmony prevails, our vibrations and sensitivity are heightened and we are able to join with those on the next plane who are reaching out to us, and who have made it their mission to guard and guide us. It is in this context that the principle of "like" attracting "like" manifests itself and we find that those with whom we are in communication are those most compatible with our innermost selves. And after many years of sittings and meetings our group had not the slightest doubt that we were guarded and guided by highly evolved and loving Beings of Light.

Notwithstanding this confidence, we were mindful of our earliest instruction that spirit communication must always be under our control. Meetings always opened and closed in prayer and guides were blessed for their presence and guidance. At other times, when alone and going about our daily business, we received inspiration and flashes of intuition which were recognised as guidance, but which at all times, were subject to our own free will. Control is always essential.

The church was thriving. It was a centre where harmony and friendship blossomed. As is so often the case in the pioneering days of an organisation, there were many enthusiastic helpers keen to increase the congregation and expand church activities. However, along the way we naturally had setbacks and difficulties, some of which, at the time, were worrying. Not the least was Peter's career move to London, and the fact that the building in which we held public services and the healing clinic, was to be demolished to make way for redevelopment. At first it seemed that we might not be able to find other suitable premises, and there was natural concern for the future. But we did not recognise the guidance we were receiving!

The hall we eventually obtained was much better and large enough to seat about two hundred people. More than ample for weekly services and adequate to hold publicity meetings. Unfortunately, being a public hall, we could not adapt it to provide individual privacy at the healing clinic - something we considered to be the ideal. It then occurred to me that by moving the clinic into my offices and allowing the four healing teams to each use a room on Monday evenings, the final part of our problem could be solved. It was gratifying that the healing teams found the new conditions congenial, and easy to work in. When we had settled, we were able to recognise that good, even betterment, had come out of a seemingly hopeless situation. Problems and troubles come into our lives that, at the time, can seem so devastating that we feel overwhelmed. But where we with our limited vision can see only the problem, elsewhere threads are being drawn together and benefits are waiting to come into existence. We can only try to have faith and accept that all experiences are for our ultimate good and that patience and trust should be our watch-word. It is no bad thing to always regard one's cup as being half full and never half empty!

The healing that took place in the new clinic was excellent. From the outset Ron had been adamant that he would not affect to have medical skills, and consequently had rejected a suggestion that he and I should wear white coats, and the other teams followed our example. He was more than willing to allow himself to be a channel through which spirit doctors could work, and he tried to disassociate himself from preconceived ideas about a patient's condition in order to minimise his part in the treatment. By setting aside his own personality and allowing his old guide and friend to over shadow him, he was able to work entirely by prayer and faith. He functioned in a trance or semi-trance state, mostly unaware of his surroundings and what was actually taking place. In this way he provided channelling of the purest kind, being a clear instrument for the passage of healing energy, without any pretension to it being in any way a credit to him or us.

It was commonplace for a patient to come into our room complaining of a particular pain or discomfort, but for Ron's hands to be directed to another part of the body where the seat of the condition lay, or a more pressing problem needed attention. A instance was when a man came with a sprained ankle but Ron's hands were taken to heal his stomach! It was only afterwards when both conditions had been attended to, that it was revealed that the patient had vomited earlier in the day.

It comes naturally to me to "mirror" patients' conditions, reflecting their aches and pains, which helps to identify where healing is required and ensures that the energy is being directed positively. Clairvoyance too, has often proved to be a vital part of healing sessions. It is not unusual to visualise something in the past or present that may be the root cause of the patient's current condition. The outward manifestation being only a reflection of the true problem. Often during healing, Ron or I or a helper would become aware of a relative or friend of the patient, who although now in the world of spirit, had come to watch the healing. This was a source of great joy and upliftment for the patient and a valuable part of the healing process.

An illustration of this combination of healing and clairvoyance occurred when we were visiting a patient in her home and she asked if we would have time to see another lady. She told us that Sue, who was cleaning in the house, was suffering from headaches and stomach pains and needed help. Of course we readily agreed and a slim, pale young woman in her thirties was called into the room. Ron became aware of her chaotic state of mind as she came in – even before she was seated. After introductions and when she was settled, we asked her to take three or four deep breaths and then whilst listening to her own breathing, try to relax. "Mirroring" her symptoms, I felt dizzy with the confusion racing through her head. However, she responded well to the calming affect of the healing and within a short time had fallen asleep. Sitting in front and holding her hands, I "saw" a young girl who impressed me as being her daughter and the source of the distress and confusion. The young girl was pregnant and her mother, our patient, had been plunged into despair and turmoil. In normal circumstances she would have kept her problems to herself, but when later I counselled her, she was only too pleased to unburden herself and confirm what I had seen. She told us that her family was living in a small house on a tight budget and she did not know how they were going to manage. She was trying to cope with three part-time jobs and was neither eating nor sleeping well. No wonder she was at her wits end and showing all the signs of debilitating stress.

At the same time as I was identifying her underlying problem, Ron had been guided to assuage her agitation by directing the healing energy to her head, stomach and central nervous system. It was whilst he was working that he became aware of the patient's mother standing to one side, fascinated by what was going on. Through Ron she conveyed her love and wished her daughter to know that she was always with her although they hadn't been able to communicate. This message, with a detailed description of her mother, was accepted with astonishment. It was something completely new! Something she had never dreamed or imagined and an unexpected bonus to the healing.

44

We were able to see Sue several times when we visited the house, and by the Grace of God were able to help her through this stressful time by further healing and inspirational counselling. Her mother's presence had made a tremendous impression. For the first time Sue had become aware of the possibility of an afterlife, and realised that there is more to life here than is outwardly seen. Although it was difficult, she became resigned to her problems in a much calmer way, without resentment, realising that they would pass and that life is but one phase after another. Sadly there was very little that could be done to improve matters materially and she accepted that the best she could do was to support her daughter in whatever way open to her, then leave her problems to God and the guardian angels who had them both in their loving care. I was able to give her literature to help her to understand this new way of looking at life. From our point of view, healing apart, we were happy to have opened a door for her.

A blend of healing, clairvoyance and counselling under the guidance and inspiration of doctors and healers so much more advanced than ourselves, can bring unimaginable relief to those who ask for help. But healers and mediums need to be conscious that they are exerting considerable influence on others through the advice and counselling they give. They should know in their hearts that they are working from the highest motives and ensure that what they convey comes not from themselves, but emanates from the higher realms where knowledge and wisdom are far superior to their own.

It is true to say that not everyone benefits from spiritual healing as there are persons who are reluctant to be helped in this manner. They may have been persuaded against their will to attend a healing clinic, but because of an innate prejudice or fear, they unknowingly create an impenetrable barrier. We have known this to appear as a sheet of grey steel between us and the patient, and no amount of love or sympathy on our part could penetrate or dispel it. We cannot be forced into any spiritual experience before we are ready to accept it. It is possible that such a patient may return at some other time in a different frame of mind, and accept the healing which is freely offered. It must be entirely their own choice. We cannot help where there is resistance, although it may still possible to bring about a betterment by sending out healing prayers. In many instances absent healing is most effective, but unfortunately, healers do not always hear the outcome.

CHAPTER 8 – THE HOME CIRCLE

The church development circle disbanded when Peter left for London, which was quite a blow although all the members continued to be healers in the clinic. Ron and I, keen to study further development, invited some of our church friends to join us in forming a group at home. These were people who were prepared to commit themselves to regular weekly attendance and most stayed several years – one, Margaret, for the whole eighteen years the circle was in existence. The meetings were focused on development of our Gifts of the Spirit, closer unity with our friends in spirit, and furtherance of our understanding of spiritual philosophy. Harmony was the keyword. A harmony that bound guides and sitters as one. There was no place for discord or envy. We were all seeking the spiritual freedom to unfold our innermost consciousness, and readily appreciated that we were only on the threshold of wisdom and understanding.

The format was set from the beginning. Ron was the natural leader and I opened the meetings with a prayer and brief address. Later, as we became more comfortable with each other, members of the circle were encouraged to say either a healing or closing prayer. It was helpful if, after the opening and healing prayers, I took the sitters into a meditation exercise. Asking them to first visualise a royal blue velvet curtain, I invited them to go through it and led them down a corridor off which led many doors. Some were closed others open, but more often than not we went to the far end. Through the last door we would emerge into a lush green meadow glowing with wild flowers. Strolling down a gentle slope sitters would be released to their own meditation. Some would continue to the bank of a clear, running stream. Others might wander into the countryside to marvel at the clarity of light, the bright colours and abundance of nature. Or they might lie on the bank where the water babbled musically over the pebbles. Here they could find peace. Others might sit or lie quietly in a far away field, breathing in pure air and listening to the silence. Or, perhaps best of all, they might drift into a meaningful vision which they would later recite to us. When they were asked to return, they would be refreshed and renewed by their timeless experience, ready for the main meditation of the evening.

It was never difficult to find a subject for meditation. I would be drawn to a book or the bible, and most times, would open a page at random and find an appropriate short reading. The reading and the meditation always seemed to be right for that evening, both for ourselves and our spirit communicators, but I never felt that the choice had been mine. This method of selecting our theme allowed us to become familiar with various aspects

46

of spiritual expression, and it served us well for some twelve years.

After that time of sitting together, and as the circle of friends on both sides of the veil drew closer, we were able to advance our meditations by dwelling on abstract concepts. Even those who normally would have found it difficult to think in abstract terms, found that Truth, Forgiveness, Beauty, Justice or other such concept, could be successfully meditated upon. This was a big advancement. During our evenings together I often had a psychic vision of a large umbrella covering the whole of the circle through which shone a golden light from above. And so it proved to be. Not only were we guarded and guided, but gradually we became united in our awareness and consciousness, and often all arrived at the same interpretation and understanding of the evening's theme. We felt very privileged.

Often during meditation in the circle, a person would intrude into the field of my psychic vision and I would realise that an entity from the spirit world had been brought for help. In the early days it was preferable to speak quietly and let the others in the circle know of the entity's presence in order to lead them into understanding how to deal with the situation. Later when someone needing help was brought directly to one of them, they were able to deal with the entity without reserve or fear. These souls were always included in our closing prayer. This easy, familiar contact with the spirit world was a normal part of our work, and visits from those who needed help were always well controlled by our guides.

We all agreed that irrespective of our individual progress during the course of the evening, the highlight was always the address, through Ron, by one of his guides. Usually a man of few quiet words, he would talk at length in the voices of his guides, often animated and at great speed. In a kindly, benevolent way the guides would add to our discussion and often gave us quite a different point of view. Invariably we were left with new thoughts and ideas to take us forward. Ron delivered all this in a trance state and whilst he was aware of what was being said as it passed through his head, later he was unable to recall the precise content. There were some evenings when it would be our privilege to be able to converse with the guide on the main theme of the evening. Tape recordings were made at the meetings, typed the same week and given to sitters, so that these precious teachings could be studied at leisure. The circle experienced guidance of the highest order and we had no doubt of the veracity and quality of what we were being taught.

Being eager to learn, we found it difficult when told by Ron's guide not to rush into matters beyond our comprehension. There was no point in infants trying to cope with sixth form stuff. But there was good reason for this advice. A pattern emerged which showed that we would be

47

given a new philosophical idea or concept that might be acceptable to one or two members, or possibly to all. It would then seem that during the next few weeks we would be marking time and not making progress. In reality, the new philosophy would be consolidating within and becoming part of our understanding, after which we would be ready to take another small step forward. In this way we absorbed our new knowledge not only with our intellect but also at deeper sub-conscious and inner spiritual levels. It was as though the flower of spiritual understanding was slowly opening within us.

In retrospect one can see that the purpose of our first meetings at Peter's house had been to lead us to know our Gifts of the Spirit and become aware of the closeness of those who have made it their work to guard and guide us. Almost from the outset I had become aware of an Arab gentleman whom I could see and with whom I could mentally communicate. His presence was made known to me by a particular facial sensation, as though I had a moustache, after which I would see him standing or kneeling before me. After greeting me with the traditional salaam of his earthly race, he would wait for me to respond, after which he would mentally impress upon me what he wished to convey. I have been aware that this dear soul has been my guide and mentor for over thirty years and probably, even before that. It has been many years since he stood back to allow an ancient philosopher to come close and impress me. A man I have only briefly glimpsed, but whose influence is strong as when I am writing this book. But my dear Egyptian friend promised he would always be on hand when needed. And so it has proved to be. His steadfastness and love have been the bedrock of my faith and have carried me through many difficult periods.

It is useful to state here the limit of my understanding in the early days of our home circle. I asserted that we humans have a spirit that existed before we came on the earth and will continue to exist after we physically die. It was plain that for an ethereal spirit to exist and function in this physical environment, it requires to be clothed in a body made of the elements of the earth plane. The physical body is that outer garment and also the temple of the spirit within. It is natural and inevitable that the body will deteriorate and die and it is then that the spirit will be released into the next stage of its eternal existence. And this process may be repeated time and time again as the spirit evolves.

A simple analogy can be seen in the incredible changes that a catapillar has to undergo to become a beautiful butterfly or moth. As one outer covering dies another takes its place, but can we deny that it is the same life force or spirit which animates all stages of the metamorphosis?

There is no break in the continuity of life. Only change. A change of consciousness and a gentle sliding from one state to another. Those who have led a selfish life, grabbing all advantages for themselves, or lived an anti-social existence whether within or outside the home, will have imposed a deep stain on their spiritual character. But where the opposite is true and they have been helpful, of service to others and tried to live by higher principles, their spiritual light will shine for all to see. Most of us are an amalgam of virtues and lighter stains; very few are so depraved as to be all bad; none are all good. The Law of Cause and Effect will determine where we will find ourselves after passing, and all will be led forward when they are ready to progress.

Our natural communication with the spirit world, and the evidence we received in church and circle, led us to firmly believe in the immortality of the human soul and the survival of individual personality. It is at this point that many rest content and seek no further illumination, thereby spending the rest of their earthly lives in a half awakened state unaware of their true identity. Those who venture to look deeper and seek to understand how our existence here fits into God's wider plan, become blessed and stimulated into living their lives with clearer vision and to greater purpose. To live in Truth, is to have faith in an afterlife and faith in an eternity wherein the human soul may progress to the Godhead from whence it came. The cycle is a natural process in which we are all involved irrespective of our religious or cultural convictions.

Our guides consistently told us that this world is a place of opportunity for spiritual growth and advancement. Whilst we enter this lifetime not knowing our purpose or the weaknesses we carry, we believe that we are born into the environment and circumstances which allow us opportunities for spiritual advancement. It is not easy to accept that adversity should be regarded as necessary for personal development. But it is certainly true that we learn more through hard times than on those sunny days when we are happy and all is going well.

Recognition of the need for the spiritual growth is a necessary prerequisite to progress, but however much effort we put into our desired advancement, it will not be possible to achieve perfection in this life span. We should not feel dispirited if at times we take one step sideways or even two back. This is part of the human condition and we will be given many opportunities to refine those aspects of our spiritual nature which need to be improved. Some, overwhelmed and pre-occupied with the pressures of material matters, may reach an advanced age before they are attracted to a spiritual pathway. Some may never give it deep thought. But eventually all will set their feet on the path, either in this world or the next, and all will work their way towards the Godhead. Time is unimportant and cannot be measured in our known terminology.

CHAPTER 9 – KNOW YOURSELF

An outing for church members to the Spiritualist Association of Great Britain in London, led to the discovery of excellent books on Spiritualist philosophy. They opened up new avenues of thought and new perspectives on a wide range of perplexities. One particular book that is still available, is a collection of teachings by spirits of high degree transmitted through various mediums, and set in order by a man of remarkable insight and wisdom. The contents are laid out as questions and answers and range from the nature of man and the nature of the spirit world, to morality, ignorance, sin, repentance, God, plurality of existences, and the natural and spiritual Laws governing our existence. It was a breakthrough in attempting to understand the deeper truths lying behind our church services and communication with the spirit world.

As with all writings on this complex subject there will always be passages or concepts which at first reading, are beyond our comprehension or acceptance. But this should not cause concern as we are all at different stages of spiritual understanding. Doubtless at some future time, a reader will pick up the same writing which has perplexed him in the past, and find no difficulty in absorbing aspects which previously were beyond him. This is common occurrence and can come as a revelation to the reader who may not have realised that he had progressed; progression being so slow and imperceptible!

However, reading philosophical books should not lead us into thinking that we know the Truth of all there is. The whole Truth is not accessible to us in this lifetime, and may never be. But such teachings may bring us a little nearer to understanding the righteousness of natural Laws, and encourage us to re-examine our ideas and attitudes towards living. It is clear that our reason for being, is to acquit ourselves in this life so that after the change we call death, we may evolve to a stage in the next life befitting our spiritual state and understanding. Whether we understand it or not, whether we follow any particular religion or not, we are all embarked on a continual cycle of death and rebirth. There will be many lifetimes, either here or elsewhere, before we obtain perfection, but in this life we can aspire to goodness, virtue and moral improvement. The laws of God are within our conscience, and are revealed to us as we gradually become more spiritually aware.

Some come into this lifetime with an innate goodness that is evident for all to see, and shine like beacons in the darkness of the corporeal world. Others lack decency or moral values, either by reason of their own spiritual ignorance, or by having been corrupted by the environment into which they were born. But all must eventually progress although it will take longer for some than others. It is after we pass through the gateway of death that we will be able to review and judge our life here. Then we shall be able to see the justice of finding ourselves raised to the degree that we made progression.

Our circle teachings, were urging us "to elevate ourselves such that we are able to gain knowledge and understanding of true life." During meditation we were able to raise our vibrations to meet with those on the spirit plane who lower theirs to communicate with us. We were told of the desirability of carrying this higher state into our daily lives as much as we were able. Not so as to be in constant contact with the spirit world, but to enhance our spirit and bring balance into our lives.

It was pointed out that if our reaction to those who acted badly against us was anger or resentment, we would have lowered our own vibration to the point where it could do us harm. We could become depressed, ill, or even retard spiritually. Instead we should endeavour to understand why the other person acted as he did. Ron's guide told us that it was not intended that in every instance we should literally turn the other cheek. He suggested that we have another cheek and therefore there is another side to the problem, and a review of that problem may bring it forward in a totally different light. He asked us to accept without question that all difficult experiences are necessary for our spiritual growth.

We were constantly reminded of the necessity to get to know and understand ourselves and our motives. It was not presented as an easy task. Any true understanding requires complete honesty from our innermost being but we are very good at making excuses for ourselves and seek to lay blame elsewhere. To be other than honest is to our detriment and cheats nobody but ourselves. It is only by recognising and acknowledging the true motives behind our thoughts and actions, that we can make any sort of progress along our spiritual pathway. The stumbling block is our own ego and our refusal to see ourselves as we really are. Such aims are not achieved overnight, neither are they achieved in months. It takes years of honest introspection during which time we should strive to live to our highest potential in spiritual terms.

Importantly, it is our duty to protect our spiritual selves by practising forgiveness and not indulging in acrimony and other debilitating thoughts and emotions that retard our progress. Envy and jealousy often creep up on us when we are off guard and it is useful to know that we can help ourselves by avoiding contentious and vexatious people who would lower our vibrations. It was Ron who first grasped the unimportance of

51

some of the things we might normally allow to upset us. It is natural to be disappointed by people and events that don't turn out as we would wish. And from time to time we are irritated and bothered by happenings which upset our plans, but looked at against the scale of eternity our moods are often caused by trivialities which should not be allowed to upset us, lower our thoughts and impede our progress.

Our aim should be to try and cultivate a calm, even existence. One where we make the most of the circumstances in which we find ourselves. If our surroundings are not to our liking and it is impossible to do anything about it, we should rest upon God safe in the knowledge that change will come and our present circumstances will pass.

We all have one thing in common although it may be buried deep within our soul consciousness and not evident to us through our intelligence. It is that the soul's basic desire and motivation is to progress ever forward and upward through all it's planes of existence. It is as natural as the acorn's inward motivation to become a fully grown oak. But we can only start to progress if we look squarely at ourselves and recognise our strengths and weaknesses.

Without deep thought we may regard ourselves as being good, kind, fair and generous, but can we be sure? Each of us seeks to justify our actions but may be deceived by pride and ego, or even lack of self-esteem. But a careful, honest review of each days activities will reveal us to ourselves. The real test lies in examining our motives for what we have said or done. Can we honestly say that we have acted unselfishly? Are we, even subconsciously looking for some form of recompense for a seemingly generous action? Are we presenting ourselves to ourselves and to others in a false light? Motive is everything and self-revelation gives us the opportunity for self-improvement.

I decided to undertake nightly introspection with the intention of trying to be honest and critical with myself. The thought took root that I need not continue to be quick tempered and hasty, although as a child it had been part of our family behaviour where tempers flared easily but without lasting rancour. Neither should I be intolerant and impatient with those slower than myself. I did not bear grudges and my flashes of irritation soon passed and were forgotten, but I was aware that others on the sharp end did not recover so quickly. The pace of my hectic life was fuelled by nervous energy and pondering on this, I realised the need for calmness and a more even lifestyle. It became apparent that an inward change to be more patient and kind was not only desirable but that I would not have to strive alone. I could reach out to those in the spirit world for their help and guidance. Heartened by this thought I prepared to take another step along the way.

Through the circles I had become aware of the guides around me but was mystified when mediums visiting the church told me of a young girl who was close to me. I was unaware of her and had not seen her in meditation, but when I met her in a dream she was every bit as beautiful as had been described. When I awoke I was able to paint her portrait in which her long blonde tresses were bedecked with delicate flowers of every hue; the picture which today stands by the desk at which I am working.

In the dream – which occurred twice – we were both dressed in long flowing white robes, and I was flying with her over a desert where the sand rippled in soft pastel shades of blue, pink and green. Flying was effortless and seemed perfectly natural. My companion and I were in complete accord until she drew ahead and I found myself lagging behind. I called to her to wait for me, but she said "Not yet. Not yet." And I awoke completely relaxed, marvelling at the happiness she had brought to me. A visiting medium told me that she had attached herself to me to learn - although I could not think what that might be. But whenever I thought of her and mentally asked for help, peace and happiness washed over me.

In this same period, my offices occupied the first floor of a building that had once been a private school and I had a delightful room overlooking an old but neglected garden. One early summer afternoon I was attracted to the mock orange tree which grew up to the open window and was savouring its heady perfume, when out of the corner of my eye I sensed a movement and a small hand protruded from the top of my desk. I stretched out my arm and gently took the warm, soft hand in mine. Behind the hand appeared the lovely face of a young girl with brown wavy hair and dark eyes that were looking directly at me. Time stood still, although it was probably only a few minutes before the hand withdrew and she disappeared. But that short time was magical in which the little girl and I seemed to exchange pure love. It was an emotional and almost holy experience that left me in a state of utter peace and happiness. Once again, I had been made aware of the nearness of the spirit world and its interaction with those sensitive to its presence.

These young spirits appeared at the right time. By bringing such peace and calmness into my being, even for so short a time, they were encouraging me towards my goal and giving me a glimpse of how much richer a calm life could be. From them I learned that control of undesirable thoughts could be attained, and was heartened to persevere towards becoming a more balanced person.

However, having decided to try and break out of a habitual thought pattern was not quite the same as actually achieving it. I was still liable to be disappointed and impatient with someone who had not behaved as I would have liked. But now I found it possible to stop what I was doing, sit quietly, and mentally tell my guides that I was more upset with myself than with the other person and did not want to feel hostile or angry. In asking for help, I was not praying to my guides, but speaking sincerely as to friends, and it never failed to produce the desired result. It was always as though the anger or irritation had been momentarily lifted from me and a peaceful passiveness had descended in its place.

This was the beginning of an important change that helped me to develop an inner equilibrium until eventually a state of serenity and contentment took over my life. But it was not easily achieved and in any case, was a long way ahead. At the time, the first important step was to face myself and acknowledge the need for change. Equally important was to acknowledge the need to be helped towards my goal. It was the beginning of a humbleness of spirit, a clearing of the decks. Time proved that change of spiritual character can follow, eventually take root, and become part of one's natural psyche.

At all times, even in stress, calmness and peace is within our reach when we realise that we have the freedom to be exactly what we would aspire to be.

CHAPTER 10 – THROUGH THE VEIL

It had become a regular occurrence for us to spend time on the Lizard peninsular in the spring and autumn of each year. These holidays were arranged so that we could visit my mother-in-law who, with our help, had left the Midlands and was now living near Penzance. It should have been a therapeutic move for her to get away from the scene of so much unhappiness, but in spite of liking Cornwall and having friends there, she was still a bitter woman. Our visits were not enjoyable, and on my part, no more than duty towards my husband and daughter. It was a particularly difficult period in my life, when in spite of good intentions, I was constantly overwhelmed by the affect her mischief making was having on our marriage. Ron carried an unnecessary burden of guilt at having left her to live alone, and although he was hurt by the acrimony that always surfaced, he never ceased to care for her. It would have been so easy for me to prevent us from going, but I felt she should not be completely cut off from our young daughter. It was sad enough that she had cut herself off from her other grandchildren by her similar attitude towards Bob's wife.

Inevitably, over the passage of time, her health deteriorated and it became obvious that she was failing not only in body but also in mind. Finally she was unable to look after herself and needed constant care. During the next few years, when she was confined to a hospital in Truro, we received several panic calls when we would drop everything and dash down, always to find the emergency had passed. One Saturday morning, however, there was another urgent call saying she had suffered a relapse in the night and would we come at once. There was no question, of course we would, but we had had similar messages before.

Whilst the car was being prepared, it crossed my mind that this might yet be another false alarm and I thought I might try and see what the situation was. Sitting quietly alone I asked for help. Without hesitation there appeared a vision of her lying in bed. But most remarkably, her spirit form was hovering horizontally above her physical body. There was nothing else in view. Seeing both bodies I knew this was a genuine emergency and her time was short. Even as I looked her spirit was being released. We set off without delay and rushed down to Truro as quickly as traffic would allow. But we were just too late, which was very sad for Ron.

There was sadness too, for his mother who in her lifetime had created so much misery for others and was the author of her own unhappiness. It was many, many years before she was brought to a healing session in our house and humbly asked for forgiveness. She left with our blessing, and I remember the gladness we felt knowing that she was making progress.

I have since used clairvoyance in this way, although not always quite so accurately, when we have been giving healing to desperately ill patients. We have invariably been privileged to channel vital energy resulting in relief from pain to a greater or lesser degree. However, there may come a time when it is evident that the physical condition is irreversibly deteriorating and all that is left is to give palliative care. It is then that we, as spiritual healers, try to induce an inner peace which instils in the patient calmness, peace of mind and even contentment. Under these conditions, during healing or sitting quietly, I ask to be shown how much longer the patient will be with us. Usually I am shown a tree from which I judge the month or season in which the person will depart. The only time this has failed is when I have misinterpreted the symbol presented to me, that is, misjudged the month. It is a truism that a message is only as good as the medium's interpretation. I hasten to say that such information has never been passed to the patient or his relatives, but facilitates my understanding of the situation and helps us when dealing with a patient's relatives.

Over the years my father had been quite dismissive of our visits to Spittlefields and had never seen reason to soften in his attitude. The family home in London had been bombed during the war, and my parents, brother and youngest sister had settled in Gloucestershire with no hankering to return to the city. Indeed, they settled easily into their new way of life, considering themselves fortunate to have been able to make such an undreamed of change in their lives. My parents had lived through two World Wars and were adaptable and philosophical people. Dad had great confidence in his own ability to cope with whatever life threw at him. He was a man of medium stature, muscular and quick in his movements. He was rarely without a ready smile and could see a funny side to most things. In later years his unruly blonde, curly hair became beautiful silver, but even in old age his smart, military bearing never quite deserted him. After years in the army he appreciated the warmth of family life and was devoted to us, and it could not have been easy when mother and my youngest sister, Valerie, joined the local Spiritualist church. The latter, in due course, became a healer. There was a thoughtful side to his nature and he was open minded and innovative where modern technology was concerned, albeit a stubborn one when it involved the Spiritualist church. Neither mother nor Valerie could persuade him to attend a meeting.

There were times when visiting them that we would take along a Spiritualist Minister who was booked to conduct the service at their local church. He got to know mother, but had little contact with dad. At other times when we visited, dad and I would slip back into our old routine of discussion and argument and inevitably this led to talk of an after-life. Dad did not concede one iota and we would laughingly end with him declaring that, "She knows all the answers!" But that was as far as he would go.

It was sad that the effects of the First World War caught up with him and in his latter years he endured considerable pain from claudication - the result of frost bite in the trenches in 1914 or 1915. But it was later, when he suffered a couple of heart attacks that he asked us for healing. Another case of a person in extremis turning to spiritual healing when all else has failed! He turned to us more as a challenge than in the belief that we could help. He almost said, "Well, come on. Here's your chance, prove it." Importantly, he did not put up a barrier and was receptive to the healing energy we were privileged to channel. Generously he did not attempt to play down the relief he felt, and readily acknowledged the existence of energies he didn't understand and had previously denied.

Some months after he had opened his mind to this new reality he was amazed to find that he was able to see his own guide, an Arab, a state of affairs he would once have derided. Here it is interesting to note that after suffering frost-bite in the trenches he had eventually been transferred to Saudi Arabia and rode in the Camel Corps with the Bedouins. It was with pride that he had received a rare medal from the King of the Hejaz for his part in the campaign that featured Lawrence of Arabia. It was a period in his adventurous life that meant a great deal to him and it seemed to me that he had a natural affinity with the Arabs; he certainly understood them.

The sighting of his own guide provoked a series of searching questions whenever we saw him and I was pleased that he gained a level of understanding so that when his time finally came, he had no fear of death. In fact three days before he died he laughed as he told us that his Arab guide and others had come to his hospital bedside during the night, but dad had told them he was not yet ready and to go away!

My mother agreed he should have a Spiritualist funeral conducted by our Minister friend. It was a beautiful, warm, uplifting occasion and paid tribute to an honest, kind, gentle man who, outside of war, had never knowingly hurt another living person. It was only a couple of months after his passing that I became aware of him standing with arms folded, leaning against the doorway of the greenhouse, watching me repot geraniums. During his time in Gloucestershire he had become a keen gardener and it was so natural that he should be there with me. Now when I have a gardening problem I always say, "Now come on Dad, what do I do about this?" and then act on the first intuitive thought that comes into my mind. Let me add, with good results!

My mother was a small, attractive, black haired beauty with

expressive blue eyes. She looked more like our sister than our mother! Her personality was quite different from dad although they got along very happily during their fifty-year marriage and were always laughing at the same small things, sometimes quite incomprehensible to others. She could be practical in an emergency, but mostly she was sentimental and lived her life ruled by emotions over which she exercised little control, declaring she could not help what she felt. I loved her dearly but have to admit that her life was made difficult when she allowed herself to be upset by trivialities and then let them rankle. The important decisions in her life were made emotionally rather than rationally. She had a personalised notion of love, duty and relationships which demanded too much from others, and often rebounded on her with self-induced stress. For many years she suffered high blood pressure, hiatus hernia, bronchitis, asthma and arthritis, none of which were helped by her over reaction to life's problems.

When she lay in hospital in a coma after a massive stroke, I asked my guides to allow me to know whether she would survive. Sitting quietly at her bedside, I was transported to a huge cavern where I saw her crossing a footbridge that spanned the right hand wall. Below was a deep, dark abyss of unfathomable depth, but the opposite wall, from top to bottom, was lined with an Angelic choir surrounded by glorious light. Mother, entranced by the sight and sound of these heavenly beings was steadily making her way across. I knew then there would be no way back. I could not understand the cavern. I disliked the dark depths over which she was traversing and it troubled me that her pathway had been potentially frightening although a firm, safe bridge and handrails had been provided.

It was some years after her death that I recalled a conversation when she had told me that the most holy moment of her life had been at my naming ceremony in the synagogue. Mum said she had felt that she was standing in the very presence of God and his Angels as she offered me up to Him to receive His blessing. Thinking about it, it seemed to me, that the angelic host and heavenly music might have been what she had expected to find on her transition into the afterlife, and she would have been without fear. There was certainly wonder in her face as she trod slowly but steadily across the bridge.

The same dear friend who had conducted the service for dad, conducted her service also, and those in the congregation who had never attended a Spiritualist funeral were impressed by his emphasis on the unbroken continuity of her life. Not continuing as someone who had been ailing, but as a new person once more in her prime. Nothing can replace a parent, there is always a void that can't be filled, but it was consoling to know that she had belief in an afterlife. I now believe she made an easy transition and had no difficulty in recognising her new situation.

In subsequent years I have not felt the necessity to visit my parents memorials in Cheltenham, knowing that no real, tangible part of them is there. I treasure the occasions they have been in touch with me since their passing, which is now very rare as more than twenty years have now gone by. I just hope that I haven't been unaware of occasions when they might have tried to contact me. I will always miss them but I know they are alive and I pray they are making good progress. And they are only a thought away.

It was exactly a year after mother passed that I had one of my visionary dreams. In it, I found myself driving across a desert where the sands stretching out before me were the same delicate pastel shades as I had previously flown over with my young guide. The sky above was cloudless. The air was warm and clear without the slightest breeze. In the distance were hundreds, maybe thousands, of people walking diagonally across my path. It seemed that I was driving from east to west whilst everyone was walking north to south towards the warmth of the sun. As I came to them they naturally parted and I drove on until I came to the edge of a town. There I made my way unhesitatingly to an adjacent apartment block and went upstairs. On the stairs several persons were loitering but they didn't approach or impede me, indeed, I wasn't sure if they had seen me as I passed easily between them. It didn't seem to be my first visit as I knew exactly where to go. When I knocked mum opened the door. Tea was ready and we had a lovely, happy, chatty afternoon but of course, eventually it came time to leave and she said she would come down to see me off. The stairs had cleared of people and we arrived at the pavement to say our good-byes. The beautiful glow of the tinted desert stretched before me and the sky and air now hung heavy in a golden hue.

Hugging and kissing her goodbye, I said "Won't you come back with me?"

"I can't," she replied ruefully, "I'm waiting for Valerie."

I drove away leaving her standing looking after me and the vivid vision came to an end.

It was only a short time later when my youngest sister, Valerie, had a heart attack. It was devastating. She was young - just fifty-one. A real beauty with glorious soft, wavy auburn hair, and notably, a ready wit. Visiting her in hospital, it was a relief to find her sitting up in bed, bright, cheerful and her usual vivacious self. She was gladdened by the fact that the doctors had advised that her attack had been mild, choosing to ignore the rider to regard it as a warning not to over-exert herself. Being a church healer she was well aware of much appertaining to our beliefs. So when I told her of my vision and that mother had said "I'm waiting for Valerie", she went into peals of laughter and said "I hope she waits a bloody long time!" Typically Valerie! She found a joke in everything! It was wonderful to find her in such high humour.

Three months after she left hospital, Valerie was lying in bed when she saw the figure of our mother standing by the window. She later told her eldest daughter Tamsin, that she was sure she was awake and had not been dreaming.

Talking to mother quite naturally, she asked "What are you doing here?" Mother did not reply but silently beckoned to her.

Valerie was stung into replying, "I'm not coming. I'm not ready yet." Shaking her head, mum sadly said, "You will be - soon." And faded into the curtains.

It was only a fortnight later that Valerie agreed to look after her four months old grand-daughter whilst Tamsin and her husband visited friends. When the young couple returned close to midnight, they found the baby had been fractious most of the time they had been away, but when she later settled, they had coffee and Valerie went to make for home. It was then they found that her car would not start and an emergency bed was made up on a settee. Some time during the night her heart failed and Tamsin was distraught to find that Valerie had died in her sleep!

Valerie had told Tamsin of her vision, and at the same time had described the vision I had experienced before her first heart attack. But I have often puzzled over the fact that I ever told Valerie mother that was waiting for her! There had been no intention to do so when I set out for the hospital. I can only believe I was guided to do so, as perhaps, there was something important to be done before she took her transition. In the event, it was only after her own experience of seeing mother standing by her bedroom window that she took steps to put her affairs in order. Perhaps there had been some uncertainty in her mind and she needed to know that mother was going to be there to meet her. I fervently hope and pray that this was uppermost in her mind and soul-consciousness when she passed so easily through the veil.

Tamsin has accepted these events as being perfectly natural, and we are both comforted to know that Valerie was undoubtedly met by mother whom she loved so much, and to whom, in life, she had been closer than any of her siblings.

CHAPTER 11 – LOVE IS THE BOND

It was great comfort to know that my parents and sister took their transition in the knowledge and belief that life is continuous and unbroken by death. Such confidence is held by countless others throughout the world according to their creed, religion or spiritual understanding, but is largely a matter of faith. Comparatively few are able to seek proof of an after-life, and indeed, many religions forbid investigation into such matters. Through our experiences, our little circle had not the slightest doubt of its existence, nor that we were in communication with those who had lived here before and passed through the veil. Naturally, we were interested in what we might call the mechanics of passing from this existence to the next. Often, when we were talking together or responding to a church member, we would come up against various questions "What happens at the point of death?" "Are we always met on the other side?" "Is there a heaven and a hell?" "Will life be the same as it is here?" "If I die through cancer, or any other illness, will I carry it with me?"

That we desired this knowledge was known to those dear guides who ran our circle and we were blessed with two addresses which helped to clarify our understanding, albeit they were delivered two years apart. It would be presumptuous to attempt to paraphrase these communications as the essence could be lost in translation. They are therefore set down from recordings made at the time.

"17th February 1971 – communicated by Scottie.

I hope our evening together will help to bring about unison and understanding of things which are spiritual. It is our earnest desire that we may communicate with you to pass on to you that knowledge from the other spheres of which, at the moment, you are ignorant. But as one transcends from one state to another, one is able to communicate back again and pass on that which has happened to them. This is only the beginning, from infancy into junior, and we will have to contemplate that which will happen when we go forward into the senior. And this, my friends, is what we hope we will be able to communicate to you later on.

This is not easy as you have learned to date. It is a long and often tedious pathway because just as you have difficulty in ascertaining that which we are trying to impart to you; we in turn, have a similar difficulty in ascertaining the information that we wish to pass on from higher spheres. Consequently we have a long chain of communication all of which is difficult to actually communicate from one to another, down the line, to ensure that in fact, you do receive at the end, that which was imparted at the beginning.

It has always been one of the failings of communication when it is handed from one to another that it does become distorted, not necessarily intentionally of course, but in fact, as we pass the word mouth to mouth, mind to mind. Each opinion adds a little of his own mind onto that which he has received and even if it is only the manner in which he states that which he knew, and although it may be word for word correct, the actual meaning imparted of course, can be changed, and this is always difficult and why in fact, you do tend to get a great many interpretations of the same thing.

One will accept that he passes forward into the next plane and in fact, he joins his own family and lives on as though nothing has happened. This is perfectly true in essence.

But of course, one has to realise that there has been a change of state and that change of state has been brought about by the individual concerned. In other words, it was his earnest desire that he did in fact, re-link with those who have passed on ahead of him. Consequently his earnest desire was uppermost in his mind which he carried forward in his transition and so he did in fact, meet those he had loved and had known in the past.

On the other hand it can be the man who has gone forward who was not so concerned with his family, as much as his earnest desire to live more of his life and his life hereafter. Consequently he will not receive a transition in exactly the same manner. He will link with someone of a similar mind who is also earnestly desiring to live life and so we go on. But although they have both transcended from one plane to another and although those planes are very similar, it is not always possible for one to see the other, simply because he may in the first instance be completely ignorant, or secondly, have no desire whatever to know.

This is why of course, when the first man communicated back he has rejoined his family and his loved ones and everything is wonderful. The other man has transcended and has gone forward and he may have gone forward with a completely false conception of his own spiritual development, therefore, he can be quite bewildered when he learns in fact, that all that he has previous learned was of no great significance.

This is what tends to happen of course, when the people from the churches pass on, the ministers and vicars. They are good people essentially, but their conceptions are somewhat misconstrued as to what happens after death. Consequently, when they come face to face with the reality so far as they know it, on the next plane, then they are a little bewildered, and do in fact, have to reconsider and reconstruct their own ideas of what life was all about."

This address delivered at speed through Ron, formed the basis of our meditation for the evening. Afterwards, a member of the group wondered whom he will meet on the other side – his first or second wife, or both? And what might happen to a husband and wife when one is more spiritually advanced than the other - do they meet on the next plane? And Scottie intervened to say,

"For a portion of a time you will want to be with your loved ones so of course, you can be, but what we are trying to say is this. That because you are now developing spiritually and are obtaining a certain awareness of spirituality – that when you pass on, if, as we expect in the majority of cases, loved ones are gathering there to join you as you pass on, you will link with them, of course. But then when you have got into the run of things and have become part of the new home again, then you will start again to think spiritually. And this is where you may leave your family, just as you left your home tonight to come to this circle, so you will leave the family to go on to develop spiritually. They can either follow with you or you will draw away from them. The love and bond will still exist between you. It is not a severing off, but you will then start to go this way, but you will always link back again and you can always return back again. You will always have a bond with them."

Exactly two years later on 16th February 1973, a guide whom we called the Vicar, opened the circle with another aspect of transition into the afterlife.

"Once again we join together with the sincere desire that we, as we circle, may link with those from the other side who are of like mind and thus attuned to those of the higher spheres. That we may, by elevating our thoughts and casting the material things from our minds, form that bond which allows the meditation of those from the higher spheres to permeate through to us and give to us that which we so earnestly desire, namely the truth of life. Surely this is what we all seek? We read copiously of the various interpretations and yet we find no satisfaction because there is no clear understanding of the transition from one stage to another. If we could but come to understand that this transition is merely what the name implies, just a sliding from one state to another. Not a sudden change in dimension other than that which is created by the new form in which one lives.

One has been told that one dies and yet one is also told that one lives, this in itself would appear a contradiction. One must therefore put it into the right perspective. What is it that dies? Only the body which has been the vehicle for the spirit. The spirit continues to live and therefore in continuing to live, it must take with it that which it has already learned, and if it passes on into a new phase then surely it takes on a new garb while it traverses that new phase. Therefore we have the Etheric Body. This is again, only a means of transportation because we still have a great deal that

63

we must rid ourselves of before we can become but purity of light.

Consequently, as we traverse these planes we do so at our own time, at our own understanding and if we wish, can continue as we have done in the past, learning very little and gaining nought. Or we can if we will, study and ask questions and seek the truth and learn a great deal from those who have passed on that much further again. And because there is obviously a limitation on how much we can learn at any one time, until we have experienced certain new facets, we are not capable of understanding something outside the known dimensions, and this unfortunately, is where the trouble commences.

Everyone is willing to accept that which can be scientifically proved in the sphere in which they dwell at that time. Anything outside those known dimensions is ridiculed and said to be absurd. So it is unfortunate because of this predicament, that it is not until one has passed into this new sphere and experienced this new dimension that one can understand and appreciate its very existence. Many have prophesied that it will happen. That someone will return again to the Earth Plane to try and explain once more of that which happens. Maybe this is so, I do not know. Perhaps it would be a great thing if it would happen, particularly if he were such as the Jesus Christ who came before, because the powers that he exhibited could have been put on trial at any time under any conditions.

Unfortunately, due to the materialism of people through many centuries, they have discarded the spiritual knowledge that they had, for the material. Consequently, the moment they are taken out of material surroundings they are unable to communicate in any shape or form, except perhaps, one or two who have the ability. This is not sufficient to prove to science that a dimension exists outside their own, and so doubt exists and will continue to exist, unfortunately.

So you have always within your mind this doubt, this "is it or isn't it" and so the only way you can hope to achieve anything at all is to take it step by step. Learn if you can, that there is another world. That this is factual because in fact, you have been able to communicate with it. That it has certain dimensions outside your own that enables a spirit, once he has discarded this earthly body, to move at a speed quite unknown to yourself. That thought has a tremendous power quite beyond that which we comprehend. That these things which have been taken and accepted as merely incidental on the earth plane, do become more and more critical as one discards the necessity of the physical part of things.

And so, my friends, let us this night try and discard all that is material and concentrate purely on spiritual matters. That we may be privileged this night to link with those who have passed on ahead, who have studied

64

and learned and because of their understanding would wish that those who will, may learn something of that which they have learned. God bless you."

So there we had it. Love is the bond, the true bond, and it is to those we love that we gravitate when we pass over. We will not relinquish our free will nor the responsibility it carries with it, and in our own time, according to our understanding, will eventually pass on to higher dimensions as befitting our spiritual state. Thus we will continue our journey from one state of consciousness to another. Each new state requiring a new vehicle to carry the spirit, each more refined than the last, until we become but purity of light. Such teaching suggests a gradual loss of individual identity as one merges with like souls in the higher spheres. This may be beyond our comprehension, and even seem distasteful, but it is sufficient for us to understand that our aim should be to live this life in the knowledge that progression of the spirit is our reason for being.

That the Vicar made reference to speed and a dimension of time unknown to the physical world, validated my understanding of precognition and a state of dream consciousness wherein one can travel forward or backward in earthly time.

I have referred to the reluctance of our dear doctor to give us his name which he dismissed as being irrelevant, and not wishing to make the same mistake again, we gave our own names to our guides derived from their particular characteristics. It was not difficult to name Scottie who had a pronounced accent. The Vicar always sat quietly, his hands clasped in prayer before he began to address us, and his manner of speaking was cultured and precise.

My own guides are the Arab gentleman who gives inspiration at all times, and helps with the healing. There is also a dear healing nun who overshadows me. She is a tiny person and when we are working together it seems that I have shrunken to her size. After any session when I have stood behind a patient, it still surprises me, when I open my eyes, to find that my head is not on the same level as the patient in the chair!

Other guides have come to us for short periods and we have named them all, one way or another! Our old spirit doctor who came to help and direct us at the beginning and refused to give his name, often brought others along to the healing sessions in the church and at home. "So they may learn," he said, " how healing works." At those times a healing session actually became a training clinic for those on the other side of the veil!

CHAPTER 12 – THE BORDERLAND

For many years I had felt sympathy for those who are suspended in the grey area between life on earth and the after-life. They may be souls who in their earthly life had no knowledge of nor belief in an after-life. Or they may be souls who for one reason or another desperately wish to cling to their former existence and refuse to recognise their new state of being. Whatever the reason, they are sadly lost and bewildered and can see no way out of their predicament.

My sympathy was put to the test when a number of us were invited by Mrs Harverd, a medium very well known in the Midlands, to accompany her to investigate some strange happenings in a nearby town. A kindly, motherly figure she had spent many years serving the churches and was at an age when most people would have retired, but she was still full of vitality and good health. She knew us well as several years earlier she had given us additional instruction on healing and she had followed our progress with interest. Excited by the prospect, we understood that ours would be a support role to supply psychic energy to increase the chance of success, but that we could participate if we saw or heard anything that might be useful. The chosen five were sitting in our development circle and hoped we could rely on our compatibility with each other, plus our closeness with our guides, to provide the strength of power the situation might demand. The medium and I were the only two in the group who had previously experienced a haunting.

We had little information to go on. Mrs Harverd had been recommended to a lady whose two teenage daughters were experiencing problems that suggested a frightening ghostly visitation. There were no details except that the girls' father was not happy we had been called in and had dismissed the whole affair as nonsense. He wanted no part of it and declared he would be out of the house on the Saturday afternoon we were to visit.

So it was that we arrived in a small, ancient country town on a bright, sunny afternoon and found the address we were looking for in a narrow pedestrian walkway between houses on the one side, and an old Norman church on the other. The three storey house was in a terrace of similar old properties and in response to our knock we were given a warm welcome by a pleasant lady of about forty. She led us up dark, steep stairs to the top floor where the girls had their bedroom. We found that they slept in a narrow attic room with a sloping ceiling and a window that charmingly overlooked the church clock. As we entered the house, Ron had seen the spirit figure of a middle aged man wearing a leather apron, standing just inside the doorway, but he did not mention it at the time.

Mrs Harverd set a large tape recorder on the table, plugged it in and checked to see it was functioning. We settled down. The mother sat on one of the girl's beds as an observer but Mrs Harverd had said it was not desirable for the girls to be present. It was then that the mother told us of various events that had led to our being called in. It was alleged that over a period of several weeks, various articles and clothes had been tampered with. Some had been moved, some had been turned round, others were found in the middle of the floor, and sometimes they had just disappeared. The crux had come when one of the girls had the terrifying experience of having the bedclothes dragged off her bed as she slept. It was then wisely decided to seek help.

The proceedings opened in prayer. Almost immediately our leader became aware of the presence of a child who regarded us with hostility and refused to communicate. It was a difficult situation and it took over half an hour of gentle coaxing before we made a breakthrough and she told us her name was Emily. Bit by bit we learned that she had lived in the house for many years, although she could not say when, and had been badly treated by her father who was strict and, she said, cruel. She told us that she was beaten when she was naughty, but sometimes she had been beaten but did not know why. She told us that one method of punishment was to be put out into the garden and be left there until it was dark which, from the way she told it, obviously terrified her. When questioned, she said she used to be put behind a shed and she would pull up plants "To show 'im."

Then quite suddenly, as if overcome, she again refused to talk, saying she did not know us. We had to patiently start again, but this time, at least we had a basis on which to build a relationship. Sympathetically we told her that she did not have to stay in this house where she was so unhappy; it was not her house anyway, two very nice girls now lived here and she was upsetting them and making them frightened. But if she would go with the two angels whom we could see were waiting to take her to Heaven, we promised that she would be very happy. But this had the effect of making her angry and distrust us more. She flatly refused, saying that her father had told her she was too wicked to go to heaven, so she knew she could not go there. And anyway, she did not know who we were and why should she listen to us? It was very sad and seemed as though we were not going to be successful and would be unable to rescue her.

Then one of us asked if she had any friends and she replied "Yes, John. He makes shoes." She added that his shop was at the end of the row a few doors away. Ron then told us of the spirit presence who had met us at the front door and I asked Emily if she would trust John, who loved her, to take her away from this house and look after her. She was pleased at the prospect of seeing him again, and agreed that she would trust him to take care of her. In the closing stages I was able to see her taken away by John and two guides noting that she was wearing a dark dress, white pinafore and boots similar to those worn at the turn of the twentieth century.

After a closing prayer and whilst we had a cup of tea, the mother told us that it had puzzled her that there was a patch of garden to the left of the back door where absolutely nothing would grow. As we prepared to leave Mrs Harverd checked the recorder and to our dismay found the tape was blank!

For a fortnight all was quiet then we got an urgent call to go back as Emily had returned, as mischievous as ever. It appeared that the girls' father had decided to decorate the stairs and was working on the top flight when to his consternation and horror, a roll of wallpaper was torn from his hands and hurled into the bedroom. It was he who demanded that we be brought back!

Emily was by turns defiant, petulant and apologetic.
"Well," she said "He didn't believe I was here. So I showed 'im."
"That was not very kind," the medium gently remonstrated. "You know you shouldn't be here. And you promised you'd go with John and let him look after you. Why didn't you stay with John and his friends? Don't you like the place they took you to? We're very disappointed."
And so it went on. Coaxing, sympathising, telling her how much we loved her until she warmed to us and trusted us.

It was during this exchange that we learned it would soon be her birthday and a member of the group asked if she'd ever had a party. Not surprisingly, she hadn't. It was then suggested that if she would be a good girl and go with her three friends to please us, we would have a birthday party for her. We promised that she would be happy in her new home and said we trusted her not upset the girls again. Once more she left with the spirit friends and we went home feeling more confident. We had not attempted a further recording as we had now learned that it was not unusual for malfunctions to take place during psychic phenomena.

A couple of months later during a normal church service, the visiting medium, who was unknown to us, said she had a message for five people in the congregation from someone called Emily. She said Emily sent her love. She thanked us for our help and wanted us to know that she was now very happy. A brief message that was so uplifting, and after the service we drank a toast in coffee to celebrate her birthday.

It meant a great deal to me to have been involved in this episode, as for some time I had been assisting discarnate souls who came to our circle for help. They were usually distressed, feeling lonely and neglected and mostly unaware they had died and were not visible to friends and relatives. Some would appear in wheelchairs still experiencing pain or symptoms of disease unaware that their pain had no reality.

Being nearer to our earthly vibrations than those of the next plane they were brought by my Arab guide so that I could explain their true situation. My work was to encourage them to leave behind all that was familiar and go forward with guardian angels who would guide them into new, happier surroundings. I usually tried to demonstrate that they did not have to sustain their disability or illness by encouraging them to leave the wheelchair and stand up, or do something they did not think physically possible. If that could be successfully accomplished, they were more willing to trust that they could go forward.

At times the work could be distressing as I experienced the pain, loneliness and bewilderment of the person brought to me. But I had complete faith in my Arab friend and knew that under his protection these conditions would be taken from me once the task was over. Sometimes rescues would be joyous affairs and easily accomplished and even tended to be accepted by the group as almost routine. The next episode however, was outstanding in the personal satisfaction and happiness it gave to me.

It was something like thirty years after the end of World War II when, during a circle meditation, I found myself in a tropical jungle. I was aware of shafts of light filtering down through the canopy and conscious of the dense undergrowth that pressed around me. With two hands I parted saplings and tall grasses in front of me and was confronted by the wreckage of an aeroplane embedded in trees and hardly visible in the greenery that grew around and over it. As I approached the stillness were palpable. Not a breath of wind or a bird disturbed the heavy silence. The tail of the plane had broken off on impact, and I found that I had entered the main body of the aircraft and was viewing the interior.

There, in the silence, several young men in R.A.F. uniforms were lounging about in complete lassitude and boredom. They were as amazed to see me as I was to see them, and one by one they got up and came to greet me. There they were suspended in time, aware they had crashed and waiting for rescue from ground troops and in had walked a civilian woman! They did not know what to make of it and crowded around laughing and asking how I had got there. It was for me to explain as carefully and gently as I could, that the crash had been fatal for them but that nevertheless, they were alive and I was their rescuer. Not that I was alone, for I could now see the guides who were waiting to escort the young crew to their new life.

It is an episode I have never forgotten, so vivid is the memory of their excitement and laughter when they realised that they had been released from their wretched situation and their eagerness to go with the guides was wonderful. My outstanding impression is that they were just young men, little more than boys. For thirty years they had existed in the borderland, suspended in a timeless vacuum waiting release, and I had been privileged to take part in the rescue operation. It was one of the happiest experiences of my life.

We might wonder how people become trapped in similar circumstances to those related above. Perhaps the " borderland" is best explained as a state of ignorance between the corporeal world and the next plane. But the explanation could be wider than that. In addition to those inhabitants who may be ignorant of the possibility of an afterlife, there are others who are held back by feelings of guilt and fear the consequences, or like Emily believe they are unworthy. Others may have died violent deaths and wishing to cling to the earth plane, are unable to come to terms with their situation. Those who believe that nothing exists beyond this corporeal world, may need loving reassurance and help before they have the confidence to face their true situation.

On the other side of life, there are spirit guides who have made it their mission to try and take these souls forward, but they are powerless when the soul is unable to recognise their presence. At times the spiritual light of these selfless beings is too bright for those who need help. It is as though they are looking into the sun and need to protect their eyes from its power. It is then that help is sought from those on the earth plane who understand the work and have pity and compassion for the plight of these unhappy souls. Regrettably there will be those who consistently refuse to recognise their true state, but ultimately a way will be found to save them from themselves. Eventually all will go forward, in their own time, which is incalculable in our terms.

CHAPTER 13 – HABITS OF THOUGHT

Heightened sensitivity becomes a natural part of our lives when we are in regular communication with the spirit world. We become increasingly aware that we are guided by those who have our welfare at heart, and experience teaches us that seemingly small events may have significance. It seems that whilst we have free-will and should always be in control of our actions, there are times when we seem to respond in an involuntary way to spirit influence.

Perhaps this is well illustrated by Ron's narrow escape when driving home one evening from the Atomic Energy Authority's plant at Harwell. An escape which he attributed to subliminal guidance. He visited the plant every Monday and delayed his return home until the traffic had calmed and he could speed along at an enjoyable pace, which in his case meant fast! En route was a short steep hill that had a long, narrow, decline on the far side of the brow. On this particular occasion, for no apparent reason, as he approached the hill he took his foot off the accelerator and gently coasted to the top. Imagine his incredulity when he reached the brow, to see a large articulated lorry jack-knifed across the road blocking his way! He always asserted that there had been no reason for him to slow up, the road had appeared clear, and yet he had responded to an over-whelming irrational urge. His action was so unusual and out of character that he had no doubt he had been well taken care of!

Recognition that similar, if less dramatic experiences, are constantly helping to shape our lives, served to affirm and strengthen our beliefs to the point where we took a step beyond belief, and let faith take over. Ron's guides often spoke of surrendering to the Will of God and we came to appreciate the futility of saying the Lord's Prayer and repeating "Thy Will Be Done" if we resented or questioned disruptive events in our lives, or the lives of others. We found strength in accepting that there is order and balance in all things, and that even disagreeable events happen for our ultimate good. True faith brings contentment whatever our circumstances, and peace to our soul. We are able to wait upon God, and regard material setbacks as a stony pathway, confident that a smoother path lies ahead. This expansion of consciousness might be expressed as being "In harmony with life".

It is not for us to see God's overall plan, nor claim to know the Truth, but it is our responsibility to seek to know the truth of our being. The group shared our faith, and together we found a definable purpose to life. Knowing that life here and in the hereafter is indivisible, our aim is to return to the spirit world more spiritually refined than when we left. We are here to undergo a lifetime of personal experiences involving countless spiritual and moral dilemmas.

It would be how we dealt with those experiences and the lessons we learned from them that would determine our spiritual progression. We realised that although some experiences may be devastating and difficult, in reality they are more than a testing ground, they are doors to wisdom and growth.

Not one of us is perfect. We are born flawed, and the circumstances of our birth – our parents, our environment, or health, may give us a poor material start. But these circumstances should not be regarded as disadvantages nor hindrances to spiritual progression. They are in fact, the right conditions for each individual soul and provide the opportunities we need to make progress and eradicate those aspects of our nature which hold us back. Individually it may take us a very long time, even a lifetime, to identify and improve our spiritual selves, or it is possible that we may be content with ourselves and choose not to be concerned.

In addition to parentage and environment, we come into the world burdened by various weaknesses that might possibly include selfishness, quick temper, or duplicity, etc in varying degrees. If these are not disciplined in childhood they become ingrained and natural to us. Furthermore, experiences and relationships along our pathway may cause us to react negatively and develop any number of other spiritually debilitating qualities. Among these we might find prejudice, hatred, mistrust, envy, pride, snobbishness, conceit, possessiveness, bitterness and desire for revenge. Or we may develop a predisposition to worry with its direct affect on our physical health. Such negatives can manifest gradually without our being aware, and are all part of the human condition irrespective of who we are or where we are born.

On the other hand there are souls who come into the world a little more spiritually developed and are examples of probity and goodness. They are to be found in all walks of life, and their light is a shining example to others. But even they are open to develop further weaknesses and may be particularly vulnerable to self-satisfaction and pride if they regard themselves as spiritually superior. It is not always recognised that it is spiritually unwise to attract envy and contribute to the downfall of those who are envious by nature. It is also unwise to provoke persons of lower spiritual development to express themselves in anger, ridicule or scorn, or in other ways that will retard their spiritual progress.

True humility of spirit draws respect and allows others to express their better nature. It takes many lifetimes to develop a refined moral character from which many flaws have been eradicated. Does it not behove us to be compassionate towards those who are still struggling with weaknesses we may have been blessed to overcome?

For change and spiritual advancement to come about it is necessary to seek to know oneself. It has to be true that where there is conceit and self-satisfaction there will be no true introspection, no self-knowledge and no advancement. Only recognition and admission of one's weaknesses and a desire for change can open the door to change. However, even the notion of changing our persona is daunting! We are comfortable with ourselves and cannot imagine being other than we are. Our friends, families and colleagues are used to us and our funny ways, and we are confronted by the thought that they may not like us if we became different.

But the changes we seek are for our betterment and by conscious control we are choosing to be nicer, kinder, more tolerant, generous and loving. If we can take the first step and travel a little way along the new pathway, we soon find that contrary to our fears, friends and relatives seem nicer, kinder and more loving to us, and people are gravitating to us and are glad to be in our company. We will never achieve all we set out to do as we cannot attain perfection in this world, but that should not prevent us from aiming high. The fact that we acknowledge the need for change and are prepared to strive for improvement, draws wiser beings from the other side of the veil closer to us, and we become more sensitive to their promptings and can take a long term spiritual view under their guidance.

Thought is one of the most powerful energies available to us. Everything that happens through human agency is preceded by thought. Medical and scientific advances, our political alliances, the world we have built around us, have all resulted from thought. This is evident in connection with material things where planning and effort are necessary to bring action into being. It is less evident with ourselves as we tend to regard ourselves as the person we have always been. In fact, what we are today is the fulfilment of our thoughts and actions in years gone by. What we think today determines and shapes our mature selves and our tomorrows.

Our thoughts govern our relationships and attitudes, and to a large extent determine the way others regard us, as they tend to take us at our own values. Habitual thoughts become ingrained and are perpetually re-creating us for better or worse. To respond to others with kindness, nurtures a caring personality. If we act unselfishly, putting another first, we will be caring. If we allow envy to dominate, resentfulness and discontent becomes part of our nature. If we allow anger to constantly erupt, we become quarrelsome. If we think fearfully, we eventually become timid and withdrawn. If we think deceitfully we become untrustworthy. If we dwell on revenge we become consumed with bile. If we allow negative and unhappy thoughts to control us, we lose self-confidence and lay the foundation for long term unhappiness.

Conversely, if our perception of the world and those around us is positive and directed by kindness, compassion and tolerance, we bring harmony and contentment not only into our own lives but also into the lives of those with whom we are in constant contact. But it is impossible to attain harmony and peace within unless we can truly forgive those who have acted badly against us. We may not be able to forget but it is within us to forgive and in so doing, release ourselves from the power of enmity and ill-will.

Repetitive thoughts create repetitive behaviour that for good or ill, become part of our identity. To break out of the straight jacket of any form of negativity requires considerable effort and patience. The first hurdle is to recognise thoughts that are undesirable, and secondly, acknowledge they impede our progress. We may need to reluctantly concede that it is desirable to cultivate a more open mind, because ideas other than our own may be equally valid. And our nature may be such that a habit can only be completely banished by being replaced with another, and in these circumstances we must ensure that the new thoughts and perceptions we allow to take root are positive and uplifting.

The key to progression is to examine our motives for what we have said or done. A review of the past day can be undertaken each night before we sleep and will help to reveal the reasons behind our thinking. We may glimpse that our thoughts are dominated by factors we have little desire to face, and it will sometimes be difficult to be honest with ourselves. We may not, for instance, wish to acknowledge that we have acted from prejudice, bitterness or greed, or that our niceness is really timidity and a desire to appease. It will take courage to face the truth of our inner being, but it is a worthy challenge if it helps us identify and acknowledge that which needs to be changed.

Honest introspection will help us develop and expand tolerance in areas where we hold strong and possibly uncharitable views. It will assist us to recognise that everyone has qualities to commend them, and if we are disagreement or have no respect for them in a certain direction, we should attempt to balance this against other more commendable aspects of their lives.

It is when a familiar denigrating thought springs automatically to mind, or an unkind retort comes thoughtlessly to our lips, that we may realise how deeply ingrained our habits are. But if we sincerely desire spiritual growth, it is encouraging to know that we are capable of the perseverance required to banish such unworthy thought patterns, and gradually replace them with others that will take us forward. We are rewarded when

74

these new ways of thinking gradually become a natural part of our persona. Getting started is not something we can put off until tomorrow or sometime in the future. The past has gone and the future is not within our reach. There is no time other than now.

The wonderful thing is that we do not have to take up this struggle alone. If we attempt to achieve spiritual betterment by sheer physical will, we are making our task harder than it need be. We must never forget that we can reach out to those souls in the afterlife, who are closer to us than our hands and feet, and whose dearest wish is to assist our spiritual advancement. We ask for their wisdom, guidance and help, and we pray to God, the Almighty Power, for strength to overcome our weaknesses. When we humbly acknowledge the need for help and allow this need deep within us to express itself, we open a door and create the conditions in which we can be influenced for good.

There are no short cuts, changes are slow, almost imperceptible, until there comes a day when we realise that we have naturally reacted to a situation in a better way than we might have done some years earlier. To know that our feet are firmly on the path and that some small progress has been made is a joyous realisation. But we should be careful to avoid creating a new thought pattern in which we picture ourselves wearing a halo – or at least, as having undue righteousness!

CHAPTER 14 – REGRESSION

Our understanding of death of the body is that it facilitates the release of the spirit into a higher rate of vibration within which it continues to function. The old physical body is completely discarded, but the etheric, or spiritual body, carries with it the mind, intelligence and spiritual understanding. The mind is still the same, it doesn't suddenly become wise, and the personality of the individual is as strong as it ever was. The etheric body will carry the spirit to the level at which it is qualified to function, which will usually be the next plane to that of physical earth and we understand it will take many lifetimes to earn the right to rise through the various planes of existence. Did not Jesus say "In my Father's house there are many mansions"?

The group asked themselves whether the spirit's future existence might also include multiple lifetimes on earth? We asked whether we might be required, or even choose, to live here again. We understand that we cannot achieve spiritual perfection whilst on earth and it therefore follows that if we return, we still will not be able to achieve it. So what would be the point? But our guides have emphasised many times, that this earthly plane is the plane of greatest opportunity to overcome that which needs to be refined or eliminated within us.

There are negative aspects of our being which often we don't recognise and may even not believe if they were pointed out to us. It is a strange quirk of nature that we often recognise our own flaws in others, as though they were a mirror, whilst not relating the flaws to ourselves. Life here is an exercise in dealing with inter-relationships, but if we wish to progress, we must allow transcendence of spiritual thoughts to motivate our actions. It is here, in this lifetime, that we have the opportunity of treating others with respect and tolerance, irrespective of their situation in life. Tolerance comes with recognising that we are all on the same path, albeit at a different stages. Not on a ladder where some are elevated higher than others, but being just a little farther along the spiritual pathway. Who are we to judge another's worth? Might it be that we have trod the same pathway as he whom we would ignore or despise? Have we indeed, passed this way before?

When therefore, we were presented with an opportunity to explore the possibility of reincarnation, five of us decided to take advantage of what we perceived to be another open door. We discussed the matter carefully and concluded that our now long experience equipped us to take such a step. It was hoped that the outcome might provide a measure of enlightenment and also enable us to indentify an underlying pattern or motive for our present life.

It would irresponsible however, to omit from this record the warning issued with the material we used. Both author and publisher warn that regression is not to be treated lightly and certainly not used as a party game. They stress that unpleasant experiences have occurred when experiments were carried out in America and London, also in Australia where the system was devised. Special steps and exercises need to be rigorously and completely carried out before the subject is put into a semi-hypnotic state. Only then is it possible to induce visions of a previous life. It is not unknown for the subject to suffer extreme distress, or at the other end of the scale, extreme happiness. However, as it is a condition of the experiment that the subject must always be aware of his natural surroundings even whilst experiencing a previous life, he can terminate the proceedings at will. This, we know, is not possible in normal sleep state. Thus we know we are dealing with visions not dreams. It is not my intention to encourage anyone to follow our example, quite the contrary, therefore I will not be giving the modus operandi, except to say that one person undertakes the task of "talking" the "subject" through the vision. He is called the handler, and his questions lead the subject into observing his surroundings. As the handler becomes more accomplished the results are more detailed; but we had to find our way.

We gathered in a warm, well-lit room in the comfort of our own home and set up a tape recorder. I was the first to undertake the experiment and my regression was short and incomplete as it touched only a small part of that particular lifetime and didn't proceed into maturity. Let me explain.

My first impression came easily, but it surprised me to find myself as a young teenage girl emerging from a large, round mud hut in what I thought might be Jordan or Saudi Arabia. Balancing a bucket of sorts on my head I walked barefoot to a nearby well. My dress was plain, made of coarse material with a rope tie around the waist. Looking to the right across an empty, rocky desert I could see blue mountains shimmering through the haze and my thoughts went out to my father who I knew was many miles away selling the goats I tended. I was sad as I knew he would not be back for some days. As I neared the well I came upon some youths laughing and talking idly in the shade of a large tree. Feeling self-conscious, I lifted the bucket down, tossed my head and swung my hips in a naive attempt to attract attention. Having drawn water I returned the way I came.

Entering the hut I noticed a small inner passage to the right which followed the contour of the outer wall and formed a recess apart from the main room. My attention turned to the room and to a young child asleep on goat skins which covered most of the earthen floor. I knew the child in my care was a sibling and as I returned to normal consciousness I realised my name was Yasmin. I was intrigued about that passage as I could not think such a design existed. However, one of the group was a sales director who spent a good part of each year in the Middle East, and he assured me that such a structure was normal and that the passage served for toiletry purposes.

I would have liked to know more about life as Yasmin but we were inexperienced and had underestimated the lengthy procedures that had to be completed before regression could begin. The whole session therefore took much longer than expected and disappointingly had to be cut short. It pleases me to know that at some time I have experienced poverty and perhaps will not have to undergo the same trial again. But vanity is still part of my psyche and I doubt if there has been any improvement. I am vain about my appearance and surroundings and doubtless my constant aim for perfection is part of the same flaw.

As their turn came, others in the group had widely differing experiences. There were varying degrees of success dependent on the subject's ability to cope with the difficult preliminary exercises. All their previous lives were quite ordinary according to the eras in which they took place, but nevertheless, seemed to bear some aspects of character which linked with their present circumstances. There were no extravagant claims to be Cleopatra, Julius Caesar, Marie Antoinette, or some other romantic figure and this made the exercise doubly satisfying. By the time my second session came round, we were used to the routine and results were more detailed.

As I lay on the carpet in front of a warm fire, the last thing I expected was to find myself as a young boy of ten or eleven years old. A grossly overweight, really fat boy! The vision opened in a school playground, where I was surrounded by children taunting me about my size and my ungainly and clumsy appearance. A figure of ridicule and contempt, cowering against a wall with nowhere to run and nowhere to hide. It was painful and distressing. I hated myself and I hated those who were abusing me. And as I wept in the playground, I sobbed to my handler as I described my torment and unhappiness. He then wisely asked me to leave the scene and proceed forward a given number of years, which I gladly did.

I became aware of a small dingy office and myself as a young man, quite portly, perched on a high stool entering figures in a large, heavy ledger. The office was sparsely furnished, only a desk, stool, wooden cupboard and a hat stand came into view. Looking round I noticed an old fashioned inkwell on the desk. Only a limited amount of light entered through a small dirty window which made the room dark and gloomy. No wonder I was wearing steel rimmed glasses. Glancing down I saw I was wearing a brown knickerbocker suit that tucked into knee length hose. When my handler asked me the date I could not immediately answer but took a few steps to the window and looked out onto the dismal scene below. It was early evening in winter. An orange haze hung over wet pavements along which hurried pedestrians hunched against the weather. It was obviously a busy town as the road was crowded with horse-drawn trams and carts. It came to me that I was in Germany, my name was Hans and it was before the First World War. I stood by the window sad and lonely and there was nothing more to say. My handler moved me on.

Moving forward five years as requested, my first sensation was of intense cold. I found myself shivering with an iciness which seemed to permeate every part of my body, although I was fully aware that in reality I was lying in a warm room. The realisation came that I could not move. My legs and lower body were trapped. I lifted my head and saw I was pinned down in deep mud by a dead horse lying across my lower limbs. I had no idea what had happened or how long I had lain there. Perhaps I had been unconscious. I only knew I felt very cold and weak. Hopelessness and despair swept over me as I realised there was no escape, and I told those listening that I was resigned to the inevitable. Hearing this, my handler asked if I would like to go through the death experience and at that point I could easily have chosen to come back. But feeling safe in his hands, I opted to go on.

Still reciting the experience as it happened and visibly shivering with cold, I told my handler and others in the room that I (Hans) was not afraid. My short life had been so unhappy that, in a way, I was glad it was coming to an end. I was not aware of the surrounding battlefield, only a cameo of mud, the cold and the horse. But the cold gradually lessened as numbness crept over me and the weight of the horse seemed to diminish as feeling left my body. I remember telling my handler how peaceful I felt. Then out of the darkness I saw bright lights just above the ground and as they approached I could see beautiful beings within. They came towards me with hands and arms outstretched and as I effortlessly floated out of the mud towards them I found they were standing in front of me. I looked down at my body still trapped and as they gently and easily led me away the scene faded from my consciousness.

There was no identifiable moment of death. No sudden sensation. Just a gentle, easy continuation of myself and a glad realisation of blessed release. It was a wonderful experience which has stayed with me and been of great comfort when someone I have loved has taken their inevitable transition.

The immediate link with my present life is my irrational fear of horses. I will make a long detour rather than go through a field in which one is grazing, even if others are walking with me. It is also intriguing that I share with Hans an interest in figurework and am happy and relaxed when doing accounting. Conversely, there is no doubt that as an object of derision Hans suffered low self-esteem and self doubt and his short existence was a painful one. This contrasts with my present life where I am personable and confident, attributes which have given me the opportunity to earn the respect of others, something denied to Hans.

But most intriguing is my reluctance to visit Germany. I could have served there in the army towards the end of World War II but refused the opportunity although some of my friends did go. Many times since then it has been suggested that we take a holiday cruise on the Rhine, but I have always rejected the idea, although I know it to be beautiful. Whilst not trying to justify this biased attitude, I have to acknowledge the influence of my father who told us harrowing stories of the First World War and my own knowledge of the atrocities of the Second. I empathise with the victims of the Holocaust, knowing that if we had lost the war I would have suffered their fate. Although I can honestly say that I don't harbour hatred, I have the habitual thought that I could not be happy in the country where such atrocities, degradation and misery occurred.

Looking deeper into my life as Hans, and assuming that I had experienced genuine glimpses of a past existence, it is possible to recognise the Spiritualists' principle that eternal progress is open to every human soul. Normally this is assumed to relate to progression in the afterlife. But what if there are circumstances when as part of our progression, it becomes necessary for us to experience other aspects of human existence?

If this is so, it does not seem unreasonable that we should endure extreme conditions over various incarnations. In the experiments related here, poverty is juxtaposed to comfortable conditions, reticence and shyness against an extrovert and friendly personality, derision against esteem, and loneliness and rejection against friendship. To have value, the lessons learned in one lifetime must necessarily leave an indelible imprint on the soul's psyche and influence the lives that are to follow.

If from my regressions I accept the hypothesis that I have reincarnated at least three times, then it is likely there are other times unknown to me when I have experienced quite different conditions. It would seem that the sum total of these experiences is manifest within one's subconscious. Hence the term 'an old soul' when applied to persons of innate wisdom, natural grace and high moral character. So much depends on how we meet with the adversities of each life span, the choices we make and what we gain from those experiences, and it seems that it might take many lifetimes to gain the insight and wisdom needed to make marked progress along our spiritual pathway

It is my belief that we do have multiple lives, although re-incarnation is not part of Spiritualist philosophy. In fairness it is not possible to say with certainty, that by the method we chose, we were able to see into our past lives. But the small group who undertook the experiment were, without exception, convinced of the reality of their previous existences. Even now, some twenty-five years later, the lasting impressions are not those of dreams but of definite past experiences. I know what it is to be a poor goat girl growing up in a harsh environment and I know what it is to be mocked, friendless and alone although these conditions are alien to my present life where I am surrounded by love and know I am truly blessed.

The experiments which covered several weeks, achieved their aim inasmuch as we experienced visions and realities of a unique kind and were satisfied with the results. In retrospect however, they were inconclusive inasmuch as whilst I know what it is to be physically and materially Yasmin and Hans, I really know so little about them. At surface level I am ignorant of their spiritual consciousness, thought processes and moral standards, although I felt entirely at home with their persona. But doubtless, within my soul I am aware of all that in the past has been of spiritual value.

As the older circuit mediums retired or passed to the higher life, there was a scarcity of platform demonstrators capable of giving in-depth addresses on the philosophy of the Spiritualist movement. Many of those now serving were good psychics and often gave entertaining performances, but there were people in the congregation who wanted more. In most cases they would have received one or more messages from the afterlife which they considered to be genuine evidence of survival, but they sought to know the implications of such communications. They were in the minority. The majority came to the services regularly and believed in an after-life, but were content to receive messages and did not seek to know more. We found that if the minority who wished to investigate further were not catered for, they drifted away or came less regularly, having become bored with the format of service.

Something needed to be done, and Ron and I agreed to run a church circle for those seeking knowledge and spiritual development. We accepted ten as being a good number which would allow each person to fully participate and progress. As usual Ron's guides were the power behind our activities and he and I worked under the same spiritual umbrella. The circle had a fixed membership as we wished to build close unity and harmony that would have been unattainable in an open circle. Harmony was not a foregone conclusion as people do not start with the same basis of understanding, and although there may appear to be compatibility there is often the odd one or two who spoil conditions by becoming envious of those who make speedier progress than themselves. In the event, it quickly became apparent that two members of the new circle were under a misapprehension as to our aims and were seeking psychic development to the exclusion of all else. After a little readjustment the circle became complete and well balanced.

Most had not sat in circle before, neither had they meditated. We commenced by encouraging them to consciously relax by easy steady breathing and to visualise warmth and sunlight. They were guided to steady the mind, sit in the silence, find peace within and hold thought forms. We gradually progressed to the same format used in our home circle - relaxation, a short guided group meditation, and a reading followed by the main meditation. Thus everyone would be meditating on the same reading but what they gleaned from it would be reflected in their individual interpretation.

It was considered important that each sitter should be encouraged

82

to interpret his own meditation in which he had clairvoyantly seen pictures, symbols or colours. Only if he was unable to do so, or needed additional insight into the spiritual meaning of his visions, did I interpret with him. Listening to the interpretations of others gave members a wider base from which to understand their own visualisations. We made good progress.

Around this time we got very excited when two members asked us to conduct naming ceremonies for their children, one a newly born baby and the other a teenager. These could be officiated by the President who at the time was Harry, and he was ably assisted by Ron, the current Chairman. The format was as laid down in the Minster's Handbook and each child was given a spiritual name to add to their own and was presented with a small gold trinket. It was a festive occasion, and the committee decided to serve wine and cake to make it complete. I recall the teenager was given the name of Peace and today she is a beautiful young woman; beautiful in body and spirit. Her kind and caring nature is particularly directed towards animals and a lot of her time is spent rescuing and caring for horses that have been ill-treated. It was a simple, moving occasion, a milestone in the church's history, and family members who attended were impressed by the warmth and easy friendship they found among the congregation.

But harmony is transient in this life of trial and experience and perhaps we should not have expected the happy state of the church to last indefinitely. In a quiet, unobtrusive way a new member joined who was to change the course of the church forever. To all appearances he was friendly, helpful and charismatic and it was quite some time before his dishonesty and deception became apparent. The first indication of his exploitation of the church's good name, came when Ron and I paid a visit to Charlotte, a long standing patient and friend, who was confined to a wheelchair with multiple sclerosis. She was living in a small three roomed flat that had been adapted to her needs and being a reserved person, had few friends or visitors.

We had been aware that for over a year, this man, whom I shall call W, had been regularly visiting our patient and several times had offered her healing, although he was not a qualified healer and consequently not a member of the church healing group. But satisfied that her condition had stabilised, she turned down his offer of help. However, we thought he was being extremely kind when he planted shrubs and trees outside her ground floor window.

On this occasion however, when we visited, we found her very depressed and it took little encouragement from us for her to unburden herself. We learned that several months ago W had tearfully told her he was in serious financial difficulties and she had handed over all her savings which amounted to £2000. She was convinced that she didn't immediately need the money and the arrangement was that he should invest the capital for her and take the monthly interest to get himself out of trouble. A few months before our latest visit she had asked for the return of a small sum and although he had made many promises she had not received a penny. He had broken many appointments to see her and had now given up visiting altogether.

She showed us scrappy notes full of excuses as to why he could not get the money. The latest said the money was tied up for a fixed period and "the company" would not let him have it. Charlotte could hardly credit his duplicity, or her own foolishness. She produced all the correspondence including his signature for £2000.

We took the paperwork along to a church committee meeting expecting them to take action as W was posing as a spiritual healer and a representative of the church. But we were met with apathy and lack of resolution. The Chairman refused to support Ron and Harry when they declared their intention to confront W and ask for proof that the money had in fact been invested. But they went ahead anyway, and of course there was no proof! W reluctantly admitted that the whole of the capital had been spent to pay off his many and complicated debts. Ron and Harry insisted that he sign a statement to that effect and obtained a promise of weekly repayments which they later ensured were met. A substantial amount was recovered until W lost his job through dishonesty and there was no way of collecting the balance, which was a little less than £500.

In the interim it had gradually come to light that he was in the habit of borrowing smaller sums from a large number of people, and was in fact, still deeply in debt. Most people are basically decent and helpful to someone in trouble, but it was amazing how many who had so little themselves readily parted with their money.

The church officers were divided, and harmony sadly became a thing of the past. Ron and I, Harry and Phyllis had over the years, meditated on and received spiritual guidance on the virtues of honesty, truth and justice, and were confident we had acted rightly. Others thought we were arrogant and high minded and not compassionate to a weak man with overwhelming money problems. In our opinion he was not only weak but also a calculating charlatan who was using the church for his own ends, and our sympathies lay entirely with his victims. We drew strength from the axiom that for evil to succeed it requires good men to remain silent.

Ron and I and Harry and Phyllis were disillusioned by the turn of events and our regard for the church suffered to an extent from which we never entirely recovered. It was evident to us that there were committee members including the President, who regarded themselves Spiritualists but were in fact spiritists – believing in the existence of the spirit world but not aspiring to live by spiritual principles or values. In spite of their position in the church they thought our ideals too lofty.

After only brief illnesses, Harry and then Phyllis passed into the higher life, and then Jane too died, leaving Ron and I without three of our dearest friends. Shortly afterwards Charlotte passed over, and Lillian soon followed. All were in their late seventies. We missed them all dearly, as we had worked closely and amicably together for so many years. It was strange to realise that we were last survivors of the original committee. The idealism and keenness of the early days had diminished. Now there was no interest in holding large publicity meetings, and fund raising had become perfunctory. Slowly there was less emphasis on spiritual teachings and more on evenings of clairvoyance. The aim was to put bottoms on seats.

The problems arising from the W affair had opened a door and it was probably intended that we should have left the church at that point, but we continued to serve as before. However, only a couple of years later another door opened to encourage us to walk away. A situation arose in which a church member was giving talks to clubs and organisations purporting to represent the church. However, she used these occasions to take bookings for private readings using Tarot cards and Ron and I strongly objected on two accounts. Firstly because everyone else gave freely of their time, whilst she was using the church to earn an income for herself. Secondly, in our view, the use of these cards involved only physic ability and gave a false impression of spirit communication, Spiritualism and all the church stood for. But we were opposed by the President and the same persons who had supported W, whilst the rest of the committee were uncomfortably silent. At one particularly acrimonious meeting, I gathered my papers and we left. I am not proud of it. But we were doing ourselves a disservice by continuing.

We were deeply disappointed by the turn of events, but did not waste time asking ourselves or spirit why we had to leave the church. We had faith and we had our home circle. Others would judge if we were unreasonable in attempting to protect the good name of the church and uphold our principles. Doubtless our own attitudes and our reaction to those who were not in accord with us had played their part in the matter and we were not entirely blameless. However, it was now possible to recognise that for far too long our dissatisfaction and unhappiness had lowered our thoughts and vibrations so that we had been living in a negative state – a backward step and hindrance to our expressed purpose to make progress. It was a time of immeasurable sadness.

At the time we had no idea that our departure would prove to be the catalyst for even more far reaching changes. For the first time in twenty four years we had time on our hands to do things unconnected with the church. We began to enjoy life in ways we had not even considered, and realised that whilst we had been so focused, our lives had been slipping away. I set about selling the company I had run for twenty five years and a year later in 1985, we retired from the business world - and many doors opened.

Some years later when the church had built its own meeting hall, a new president and committee invited Ron and I to be guests at the opening ceremony, and we were touched by the many tributes to our service to the church and healing clinic.

It pleased us too, that mention was made of the sterling work and devotion of Harry, Phyllis and Peter – the latter, although relatively young, had also passed to the higher life by this time.

We had always regarded healing as the most important and satisfying aspect of our church work. It was a privilege to allow the doctors to work through us, and even at the end of a full day at the office we never felt too tired to give ourselves over to three hours or more at the clinic. Now, although no longer attached to the church or healing clinic, we found that old patients visited us at home, and more came by way of recommendation. Others just arrived!

There was the case of Florence who had recently started to work in our house, and confided that because of a chronic chest complaint, her husband was spending all his time in an armchair, depressed and devoid of energy. She asked if we would pay him a visit. When we did we found him quite depleted, and his chest was certainly in a bad way and his breathing shallow. We gave these conditions our attention and also did our best to raise him from his depression. A couple of days later, a delighted Florence told me that there had been a surprising side effect on the night of the healing - they had made love for the first time in years! I almost expected that she would require us to see him on a regular basis, but she didn't mention it again. And I certainly didn't feel that I could!

We found that those who came to the house for treatment were somewhat different to those at the clinic. They had more need of counselling and we now had time to explore the underlying causes of their condition. The counselling usually came from Ron's guides during healing. But if we were having a cup of tea later, it would not be uncommon for Ron to be overshadowed by his guide who would intervene in the conversation to speak to the patient. This could be a little disconcerting when Scottie spoke in his broad accent! At other times I would be inspired to add to the counselling, so that we worked together as one. In this way we were often able to introduce our patient to the need for spiritual awareness and unfoldment. It is fair to say that never at any time did we discouraged patients from seeing their medical practitioner, emphasising that we were acting complementary to the medical profession and not as an alternative.

Whilst healing was our first love, the exorcism we had been privileged to do as in the case of Emily came a close second. We had been involved in another case whilst still with the church, and felt that past experience and our knowledge of rescue work, qualified us to deal with a case brought to us by Margaret. She had been a member of our circle since its inception, and had been in the group connected with Emile. Margaret was still a regular member of the church's healing group. She didn't have a clear idea of the problem we would be investigating but judged that help was genuinely needed and we agreed to assist. She made all the arrangements and assembled three others whom we knew, but had not previously sat with, but we thought would make up a strong team.

It was to be the first time we would work as an independent group, but we had faith we would be well guarded by our own guides. Furthermore, I was determined not to consider we had been successful until I had seen the troubled entity, if there was to be one, taken away by guardian spirits. We judged that the group would have the psychic power and spiritual strength to meet whatever or whoever would challenge us.

We all met in a pretty country town on a clear, bright summer day, and made our way to a building that had undergone an imaginative conversion into up-market apartments for retired people. We were met in the reception hall by a well groomed, charming lady in her mid-fifties.

"Hello there," she greeted us. "So glad you were able to come. I do hope I'm not wasting your time, but I really do think there's something very peculiar going on." She hurried on. "This is the best apartment in the complex, and yet I can't sell it. It has the most wonderful views. Everything one could wish for. But buyers are just not interested and my staff won't go up there! And I can't honestly say I blame them."

She went on to tell us that there was no disguising the cold, clammy atmosphere on the top floor. Potential buyers could not exit fast enough. Nobody had seen anything unusual and there was no proof of a haunting, but she was a sensitive and intuitively knew that psychic phenomena was involved. Knowing Margaret was a spiritual healer she had asked whether she knew where to turn to for help.

We were shown into the residents' lounge which was very luxurious and later as we travelled up in the lift, I could not help thinking how fortunate the residents were to be able to retire in such comfort. The apartment was a penthouse on two floors. We passed through the kitchen and made our way to the sitting room above where a circle of six chairs stood ready. We were struck by the room's dank atmosphere and the fact that it felt much colder than below. Notwithstanding the large window and beautiful view, the room was distinctly uninviting. We joined hands and I opened with a prayer that we might, by the power of Love and Grace of God, be able to help whoever was troubled and in distress, and that guardian angels be present and visible to us. We knew that without their presence we were powerless.

Immediately the prayer was finished I felt deep sadness and despair. A sob arose in my throat and spread to every part of my body. I wept in sympathy with the emotion palpable within the room. Holding tightly to the hands on either side of me, and drawing strength from the group, I shared the loneliness and unhappiness of an old man I could see crouched in the far left hand corner of the room. I could see his face and was able to communicate that we were there to help him, and although I could not hear his voice, learned inspirationally that he was lost and trapped and had no idea what had happened to him, nor where he was. I told him we understood, and of our sympathy and love. I told him that he was lost because he no longer lived in this world, and rightly belonged to a happier place. I said we had come to help him and that he would soon be able to leave. As I spoke, two guides appeared in the centre of the room and reached out to the old man. He looked up, effortlessly arose, and without looking at us went with them to the outer wall through which they all passed taking the cold, disagreeable dankness with them. It was remarkable how quickly the temperature rose and the room became warm and even brighter. Ron told us that during the time I was communicating with the entity he had seen several spirits standing around the outside of our circle helping with the proceedings. When we closed in prayer we were happy and elated with the outcome. It was a wonderful experience. So quickly accomplished because of the victim's desire to be helped and the power radiated by our spirit helpers. There were no further problems – one visit proved effective.

We enjoyed this work. It had such important purpose and achieved so much. We recognised there might be reluctance on the part of the entity to stay in the new unfamiliar surroundings to which they had been taken, and that they might return to the scene of the disturbance. Free will always applies. But we were willing to make more than one visit to get a satisfactory result.

In all cases but one, we were blessedly successful. It was a particularly sad case involving a stableman who had caused the death of a little girl when he set fire to a stable. The stench that accompanied this presence was horrible and most offensive, and at times the room in which he manifested was made uninhabitable. This was in spite of the present occupant being an officer of a local chapel who said daily prayers in the room. When we were called in there had been an unexplained fire in a shed outside the kitchen door and the occupants had become very alarmed.

On this occasion Ron, Margaret, Hazel (the occupier who was a lay preacher) and myself sat in the small room and the stench receded as we opened in prayer. I saw the man sitting on a bricked floor in a corner of the stable, dejected and alone. I also saw the young girl with long dark, curly hair, dressed in a high necked white dress, sitting quietly on a window seat in a panelled room. There was an air of resignation about her, and when the time came to leave she obediently went with the guides without a backward glance.

In contrast the man presented us with great difficulties. He was inconsolable and consumed with grief and guilt. In his anguish he could not

89

believe that he would not be severely punished and was afraid to leave and face what he thought might await him. We made several visits during which we were able to communicate with him, and although each time he agreed to go with the guides, and in fact did so, he always returned to the stable. It was most distressing for the occupants of the house who eventually called in a vicar who said prayers according to the rites of the Church of England. Unfortunately, this was not only unsuccessful but actually made matters worse. After a gap of three weeks the unpleasantness returned stronger than ever. The stench arose whenever the owners sought to use the room for whatever reason. It became more frequent and obnoxious until the room was uninhabitable. Finally the residents under deep emotional stress, were driven out and obliged to move away.

We thought that we had failed because we could not get together a group strong enough to deal with such a difficult case. Conversely, the guides had responded to us, and on each occasion took the entity away, so that ultimately one is led to the conclusion that the free will of the entity was paramount.

However, on checking data for this book it has come to light that after moving from the house, Hazel discussed her reasons with an elder of the chapel to which she belonged. He told her that the land on which the house had been built, originally belonged to the Church of England who sold it for property development. In so doing they evicted a gypsy family who put a curse on anyone connected with the church who might live there! Hazel did not ask if there had been a fire or if a child had died. One could speculate that the gypsy's hatred and hostility against the church played a large part in the haunting. But there is no denying the revolting stench witnessed by many, the unexplained burning of the shed by the kitchen door, nor the two entities Margaret and I saw. Hazel has since visited the new occupants and was delighted to find they are comfortable and happily settled.

Experience has shown that only deep, sincere sympathy and pity, without revulsion or fear, can be successful in this work. It follows that selection of members for a rescue group is critical. Motive is everything. A person should never be included for sensationalism or because he is related to another member of the group, or because he thinks he has a right to be there. That person may be more likely to draw and absorb power than contribute to it. A long association with the spirit world, knowledge of one's guides, empathy with others in the group, humility of spirit and sincere desire to be of service should be the criteria for inclusion. It might sound a tall order, but then it is not the work for everyone, and should not be undertaken lightly.

Just as we had found that our healing work had taken on a new dimension, so we also found that the teachings at our Wednesday home circle had become more profound. Our discussions after coffee ranged on often until quite late and our spirit friends stayed too! It was by no means unusual for Ron to be over- shadowed as his guides intervened in our conversation to add their wisdom to our conversations. Many times I had to remove his coffee cup or take a burning cigarette from between his fingers as he slipped into a trance and became quite unaware of us. These interventions were greatly valued and often the highlight of the evening. We well understood that although a measure of what circle members said was inspired, mostly they were expressing their own understanding with their finite minds. We were learning from spirit and each other, but from time to time had to be reminded that we were propounding ideas and thoughts as though we knew them to be the Truth forgetting that the whole Truth cannot be expressed, and anyway, is beyond human comprehension.

It may not be generally understood that philosophy and messages from the spirit realms, in translation, may become tinged by our mortal mind and our own thoughts and spiritual understanding. This had been pointed out to Ron by his old guide in the early days of our circle when he was still trying to come to terms with his mediumship.

At the end of an evening when he had conveyed a long philosophical address to the circle, he had asked, "How do I know that what I am giving off is really from spirit?"

The answer came, "When you first start in mediumship your messages will be 20% us and 80% you. Later as you progress the messages will be about 50% from both sides, and later still when we can communicate more efficiently is may be 80% us and 20% you. When it is 100% you will be on this side with us!"

A touch of humour much appreciated by Ron, and he never tired of reciting it. It taught us to be aware that it is difficult for guides to get their messages across, being dependent on the ability of the medium to interpret that which is given.

A further difficulty arises when we try to intellectualise spiritual ideas and concepts, but true understanding will come from our soul consciousness not from our intellect which at times may try to dominate our understanding. This was emphasised by the powerful guiding spirit of Reg, one of our members, who urged us not to be misled by the mortal mind.

"Which," he said, " is a collection of those things and emotions from within the mortal frame. Our brain is but an instrument which will decay and die along with the physical body. It is easy to mislead ourselves, to think we know a wonderful truth, when in reality we can only understand according to our awareness and spiritual consciousness. That which truly IS, is beyond the mortal mind." He went on, " One may read great spiritual philosophers and the holy books, but guidance will come not from the words but from the silence between the words. That is the way of Truth. Listen, read. Ask for guidance to understand the spiritual nature of the words. Greater understanding will then be yours. Only you can do it and whatever you learn you can only express to a certain degree, because that which you know from within yourselves you cannot pass on to another. They must find it for themselves – certain things, yes, to a degree, you can express, but only to a degree. That which is a feeling and a love expressed from within yourselves, from your own being, cannot be given to another. They must find it for themselves."

He continued, "My beloved friends, we ask that you accept that which has been said with understanding, with warmth and with love, because it is our intention to pass on to you that which is purely love – the warmth of love and wisdom. We are also limited to the language that you speak. But surely you can feel the warmth of Love as it is passed on to you." His final words on this occasion were, "May the blessing of Almighty God be with you all. When you go forth from here understand that we are always with you if you wish it, giving you guidance and strength. We ask only that if you wish it, you acknowledge it, and we shall embrace you with so much love and understanding. Go forward my beloved friends on your pathway. Know that you are guided with Love and great blessings. May God be with you."

Our guides were telling us that we were only in the infancy of our understanding, and this was so and still is so. But I had come to realise that the Almighty God to whom I prayed and who I thought of as being the mind, wisdom, power and energy behind nature and the universe, and the universes beyond, is nature and the living spirit, power and wisdom within all manifestations. An energy beyond mortal mind that dwells within all creation whether animate or inanimate.

I began to truly understand that man is more than a human who has a spirit, but is the spirit. A spirit being who is clothed in a temporary physical body made of the elements of the earth plane in order to live its life here. In the past I had often spoken to others of how the spirit which has animated the physical body goes on to live in a new dimension, and thought I understood. But the full impact of the realisation that we can never be more spirit than we are now, was an awakening! It was then that I understood the Truth of my Being. The truth that I am not the person I thought myself to be.

As God is the spirit, love and wisdom in everything, it follows that this must include me and every other living soul. I now know from the depths of my being and with complete clarity, that I AM a spirit. I am more than I ever thought possible in this lifetime. But I am as nothing except as I am an expression of God's spirit. The Truth is that an infinitesimal part of God IS our True Self and thus we cannot be separate from God, although we may turn our consciousness away from Him. That I am part of God's spirit gives me all the strength I need, and I have begun to release myself to the understanding that God IS, therefore I AM. I AM part of God and God in Truth is my being.

To be human with a spirit dependent upon the physical for growth and development, is separation. To BE the spirit with a shell to convey it through this life, is oneness. It is oneness because everything that is understood and expressed by the spirit is reacted to by the body. Our thoughts and attitudes reflect our spiritual state. And conditions of "disease" can be fostered and sustained by our thought processes, however much we may protest to the contrary. We are the centre of our world and our perception of the world stems from our thoughts and the degree to which we allow our spiritual self to be expressed.

Many of us are prone to allow small irritations and set-backs to disturb us so that we habitually grumble, or even to the extent that we suffer unnecessary anxiety and worry. There is a need to cultivate calmness and tranquillity, acknowledging that every day problems are often blown out of all proportion to their importance. If we are to progress we should recognise the need to protect our true self from debilitating and retrograde thoughts. Our aim should be to maintain spiritual serenity. The desire to bring positive values to the fore in our lives is a step towards providing a channel for spiritual expression. When we allow the Big I, the Divine I, to express itself, we begin to create balance in our life – balance between the spiritual and physical. Even the smallest step towards this harmonisation is a doorway to inner peace and self esteem.

It is the mortal person, the Little I, who lets us down. It is he who allows our flaws and weaknesses to surface and the darker side of our nature to show itself. It is the Little I who lapses into despair and asks why God has allowed misfortune to befall us and those we hold dear. The Little I lacks faith and forgets that we cannot see the whole picture. Neither can we see the doors of opportunity waiting to be opened farther down the road. It is the Divine I who has the spiritual strength to trust that everything that happens is for our ultimate good and that we are always in the right place at the right time. In other words, we begin to accept the wholeness of "Thy Will Be Done."

It is proper that we should use the intelligence, gifts and skills we inherited at birth or have acquired through study and diligence. It is also proper that we make the most of our material opportunities, providing that we are not harming others by the way we attain them. At the end of the day, all our earthly ambitions and all our material achievements assume their real importance when we have the insight to realise that our true success will ultimately be measured by the extent to which we have gained knowledge of the I AM within, and allowed it to express itself. This can only be achieved through deep soul consciousness. We carry perfection and Truth deep within us, waiting to be gradually unfolded and released to free us from the Little I we thought we were.

The danger is of course, that when we attain a measure of understanding we may begin to be a little egotistical and self-satisfied, maybe even thinking ourselves superior to those around. But that would be contrary to true spiritual development and show that we are not really allowing the Divine I to express itself.

Recognition that God is the centre of our being allows us the opportunity to appreciate that He is also the centre of every other being. We are all souls on the great pathway although at different stages of consciousness and we are united in spirit. To quote St. Paul "Now there are diversities of gifts, but the same Spirit. And there are diversities of operations, but it is the same God which worketh in all."

CHAPTER 18 – TRANSITION

I stood at the kitchen window watching Ron trudge up the garden to empty a box of lawn cuttings and, once again, could not help noticing how slowly he moved. In his youth he had been a keen walker, and in recent years we had been dancing at least once a week, but his tall, slim figure was now thin and stooped - his vitality gone. Lately he had been short of breath and we had begun to sit out at dances. A blow to our pride! But there was no mistaking the change that had taken place and the fact that he had aged rapidly. Two years earlier our home circle had closed for what was meant to be a short break, but we had not reopened. We were not sure why, we only knew it was not the right time and waited for a sign to begin again. But it had not come. At about the same time the number of patients for healing became fewer, but when a case came the healing energy was a strong as ever.

We were leading a full social life, but it came as no surprise to those who knew me, when after years of retirement, I was drawn into local politics. I had always been energetic and occupied in so many directions, that I needed little encouragement to become involved in village matters, the Parish Council in particular. It was a time when there were difficult problems on hand and it was interesting and fulfilling to steer matters from the Chair.

Although we were content with our life in the village, when I saw Ron dragging himself around the garden, I realised it had become too much of a burden and tentatively suggested we leave. He obviously had been thinking along the same lines as he unhesitatingly agreed, although we had spent twenty six of the happiest years of our lives there. We thought we might move to a small riverside town, relatively unspoilt, and with all the amenities two elderly people might wish for. And as an added bonus it was only half an hours drive from our present village and friends.

The day after having our house evaluated we visited the town where we hoped to settle; saw two properties and chose one that was perfect for our needs. We put our house up for sale the same day and within six days of having our house valued we had sold it and bought the other! It was yet another doorway, and if ever we were guided, this was surely the time! The move was painless, and with plenty of professional help we were soon shipshape and a small garden had been transformed into three easily maintained patios. Although it was not actually said, we both knew that I would be the one who would have to look after them and everything was laid out accordingly. Ron was enthused by designing and creating such a pretty retreat that his energy levels picked up and he enjoyed every minute of it.

The move proved to be exactly right in every way and there followed a year of contentment and happiness during which Ron relaxed and produced some of his best animal drawings. Then the Law of Cause and Effect from which there can be no escape, came into being and the blow fell! Most of his life a heavy smoker he had not stopped soon enough, and we found he now had lung cancer and emphysema! He went through radiation treatment followed by a wonderfully happy summer, autumn and winter of remission. Then the awful invader took control again.

Our belief and trust in God never wavered. Somewhere along the road we had both attained complete Faith, although it had been a long road for Ron who had begun his journey as a die-hard sceptic. He had always believed in a supreme God, an Almighty Power, but as a young. man had scorned the concept that we might live on after death. Gradually he had progressed from acknowledging that an afterlife might exist, to the deep conviction that it actually did. As our interaction with the spirit world had widened and deepened we had both developed a complete and abiding Faith. Faith in the existence of an omnipotent power of whom we are part and who is part of us, and expresses Himself through us. Faith that we are spiritual beings in transition. Faith that the only substantial thing about us is our indestructible spirit. Faith in life eternal. When talking to others about the afterlife, with wry humour Ron would say, "I know it is true. If I am right, you won't know. If I am wrong, I won't know." But he was wrong on both accounts!

We spent Christmas 1997 in Wales with our daughter and family, but it taxed his strength and he knew he would not make the journey again. His decline was rapid and it was pitiful to see him become a shadow of his former self. He did not complain but from time to time when he was uncomfortable, he asked for relief which blessedly, I was able to channel. Quite suddenly he was taken into hospital and although I visited every day I was unable to see a consultant or doctor. On the sixth day I sat down quietly at home and asked to be shown how long it would be before he would take his transition. In response I was impressed with a picture of the plum tree in our garden and concluded he would leave in August when it would bear fruit. It was now March.

On the eighth day I was able to see a consultant who confirmed my worst fears that Ron only had months to live and suggested the next step would be a hospice. I told him my preference would be for him to come home where I had already made provision and could get assistance with nursing care. When I suggested that the situation might go on until August, he replied, "No. Some months, but not as long as that." I told him that if

Ron got to know the cancer had returned, he would not wish to live. Later that day Ron said how wonderful the nurses were and asked me to bring them some chocolates.

He was very quiet and lethargic the next day when I put the chocolates in the nurses' rest room. A young Houseman was doing his rounds and I suggested to him that Ron was under deeper sedation than the previous day and he agreed that tomorrow the drugs would be administered in smaller doses. I took the opportunity of checking on Ron's condition and was told that he had weeks to live. I told him too, that if Ron knew the cancer had returned he would not wish to live.

Ron had said very little to me that day, but suddenly he called the doctor, and in a strong voice asked him the pertinent questions. "What is wrong with me? And how long will I be here?" The doctor started to explain that sometimes cancer returns but before he could finish Ron closed his eyes and sank back into the pillows. He did not speak again and at six o'clock I kissed him and went home before it became dark.

The same evening – just before ten o'clock, a nurse 'phoned. She said, "Ron says he's going to die and he wants you to hold his hand."

Stunned, I phoned our daughter and then a taxi, but the nurse immediately 'phoned again to say she was coming to pick me up. I presume Ron had told her that I had not driven in the dark since having had two eye operations. I don't remember much about the journey. I think I chatted inanely. I know I asked if she thought he was going to die and she replied that she didn't know. But when we got to the hospital she dashed out of the car, saying we might be too late. I was in a turmoil as we ran down the corridor and suddenly, in the half light, I was faced by the bed which only four hours earlier I had left in a well lit ward, but was now enclosed in curtains. I looked in to see a nurse sitting holding his hand, and as I took her place he started to whisper the most wonderful and loving things. Words too precious to repeat, but which I hear over and over again in his soft, sweet voice.

"Ron," I asked through my tears, "why are you doing this?"

"I am only going a little way down the road," he reassured me. "you know what it is all about." Then he added, "I'll never leave you, not in this world or the next."

He denied he was being brave and courageous, and simply whispered "Not at all. I am happy and content to go."

Not wishing to disturb his peace of mind and to help him make a quiet transition, I sat holding his hand until our daughter and son-in-law arrived at midnight. At first he did not recognise them and asked who they were, but after greeting them he again relapsed. Sometime later, when his pulse was erratic and weak, he raised himself up and grinning broadly, waved towards the bottom of the bed.

"Who is it?" I asked.

"Ron and what's his name."

He never could remember Bill's name. When in the past he had spoken of them, his old teenage friends were always "Ron and what's his name." He was so pleased to see them, and I put my head down onto his arm and prayed in thankfulness. Time passed.

Suddenly I was aware that I was flying above a car that was swiftly making its way down a winding road. I knew Ron was inside. I kept pace with it from above as it wound its way through patches of bright sunlight, and then into areas of shadow cast by trees on either side. We were travelling together. A tunnel appeared ahead, and I thought "We'll go in and see a bright light ahead." But even as the thought entered my head, I was pulled up at the entrance and was not permitted to go any further. He went on and it was perhaps, some twenty minutes later that his weary body drew its last breath. When we left the hospital in the clear, grey light of dawn, a blackbird's song filled the chill morning air. Later in the week I noticed the plum tree was in full and radiant blossom.

I knew from the outset that his passing had been a blessing. He hated the indignities of hospitalisation. But the final part of his illness had been brief, and his stay in hospital only a matter of days. Blessedly he had been spared much of the pain and agony associated with his condition. His passing had been as he had lived, quiet, gentle, dignified and full of concern for me. He was a man of utmost integrity, one of nature's gentlemen and it was a privilege to have known him.

His cremation was conducted by a Spiritualist Minister. A lovely lady, sincere, sensitive and compassionate with whom I found instant empathy. It was a wonderful service during which she presented me with two roses from Ron and three years later the dried flowers are still in a vase!

CHAPTER 19 – AFTERMATH

Ron made his transition at the end of March and on 1st June, just two months later, two friends and I visited a Spiritualist church where we were totally unknown. The medium proved to be a gifted young man who at the very beginning of his demonstration of clairvoyance was almost overwhelmed by Ron. Through him Ron gave the names of people he had newly met, including my sister Valerie and our dear friend Jane. He came through in the company of a boxer dog which was an excellent identification as for several years we had bred and shown the breed and were extremely fond of them. I was startled when the medium said I should get out Ron's diamond ring. I had completely forgotten that he had put it away when his fingers had become too thin for him to wear it. But now I wear it continuously and am comforted by the psychometric warmth and comfort it generates.

The medium went on at length to convey messages about other private and evidential matters. He was an excellent channel, but admitted to being puzzled by Ron's reference to a thunderstorm. It was a long message that came over with strength and enthusiasm and Ron was obviously delighted to be able to come through. I think he would have gone on and on, but the medium said he had to break away to allow other spirit communicators to come through.

Later I was able to tell the demonstrator that at the crematorium, after the large congregation had packed into the chapel and the coffin was about to be unloaded, there had been a sudden tremendous clap of thunder seemingly right overhead. Afterwards I was told that it had amused those inside who had jested knowingly, "That's Ron - letting us know he's here." In fact, the thunder was immediately followed by a heavy deluge that heralded the floods that swept through the south Midlands in April 1998.

After his passing there came a feeling of deja vu as though I had stepped back over 50 years to the early days of our marriage and was again living my life in the slow lane, dragging out the days, waiting for him to come back from overseas. Fifty four years of marriage to one person is a very long time and reality only came gradually. I drew on my confidence and faith that death is part of a natural cycle, and rebirth follows as surely as spring follows winter. My strength came from knowing that our separation is only one of blindness on my part. He is out of my physical sight but psychically impinges on my sensitivity and I am very much aware of his presence. There is the added comfort of knowing that on his transition he discarded his diseased shell and laid down the burden of his physical being.

We were two different sorts of people. He slow, thoughtful and reserved, myself quick, intuitive and outgoing. In the beginning this caused irritation and problems arose from these totally different ways of approaching material matters. In later life he became disillusioned with new age morality and society, lamenting the loss of traditional standards and values. I would like to think that I have grown more tolerant, not only with age, but by appreciating that society changes with each new generation. However, we both agreed that one of the most troubling aspects of modern society is the growth of freedom without responsibility.

When, however, it came to spiritual understanding and faith in the unbroken continuation of life, there was absolutely no difference between us. We had been fortunate to have spiritually evolved and progressed together. We were two sides of the same coin; blessed to have found our soul-mate in this lifetime.

Of course I miss him and realise I am no longer the first person in anyone's life, but self-pity would be self-indulgent and non-acceptance of God's will. There is still so much to be grateful for with good health, spiritual strength and spiritual guidance topping the list. Every day I thank God for the sensitivity that allows me to be aware of Ron's loving presence. He is often with me - always when I am channelling healing. There was an occasion when it was wonderful to see him kneeling on the opposite side of a patient and ministering in his usual way. At other times, his hands have closed over mine and I have felt a surge of healing energy. When I caught a brief glimpse of him sitting in an armchair he looked fifteen years younger! His presence around me is very real.

Recently when I was looking through his drawing materials I found two slips of paper on which he had written:

What is Faith?
Faith is the substance of things hoped for,
The evidence of things not seen.

and,

I rest in God today – and let Him work in me
and through me, while I rest in Him in quiet
and perfect certainty.

I do not feel the need to attend church services, but on the odd occasions when I have done so, communications have been strong, long and evidential. On several occasions Ron has appeared to Christine who commenced her training in our home circle, and is now an international medium. She felt and saw his presence when she was recently demonstrating in Australia and said he was delighted to be "working", which we both took to mean healing. On one occasion Margaret too, has been aware of his nearness during healing.

Twenty three years ago, the night before the younger of our two grandsons was born, Ron and I were talking with our daughter and her husband about the coming event, when the Vicar overshadowed Ron and joined the conversation. He told us that the child to be born was a very special soul and of the mixed emotions that were accompanying his birth. There was, he said, sadness in the upper realms at his departure, although gladness too, that he was about to take a special journey. The Vicar concluded by saying that when "his instrument" (Ron) progressed to the other side of life, his gifts would pass to our daughter.

During the summer, a few months after Ron's passing, my son-in-law was walking in rough country in the Welsh hills and chose a path covered in loose shale. For some reason he had neglected to wear suitable boots and he slipped and fell breaking his leg in two places above the ankle. It was a serious accident for such a heavily built man and of course he received hospital treatment and was confined to bed. But recalling the prophecy, our daughter placed her hands over the injuries and asked Ron to help. Both she and her patient immediately became aware of the heat and healing vibrations that emanated from her hands. She continued to give healing sessions and from the speed of the healing process, it is possible to say that blessedly, she too is a natural channel to relieve pain and promote healing.

And so doors continue to open.

I have come a long way from the beliefs of my childhood, but am grateful to have been taught by my mother that God is accessible to all. This has been the bedrock of my understanding although my conception of God has changed beyond measure. It has not been necessary to discount my father's view of evolution and the world. With modern learning techniques it is possible to witness and concur that animals and plants are equipped to adapt to a gradually changing environment, and are capable of evolving into more sophisticated forms. It is man, the ultimate predator, who in his greed and thoughtlessness, is the most likely reason why other species become extinct.

Today, I believe in a supreme spiritual omnipotence and energy, whom we may call God, by whose power all things are manifest. Under this umbrella Darwin's theory of evolution is part of the natural order, as is growth of modern technology. It is inevitable that man's intelligence and ever expanding higher education, will lead him to discover energies and forces that are already in existence waiting to be revealed. Most may be used for the betterment of mankind but so often are applied to power, enmity and destruction. It is becoming recognised that man's ability to discover natural energies and harness them to new world technology, often outpaces his moral and ethical judgment.

Thus science, although regarded as being exact at any given point in time, and setting its own standards, is always expanding its knowledge and revising its absolute. In western culture, scientists have held sway for well over a century, not giving credence to anything that cannot be proved to their own criteria and generally within the confines of their laboratories. It is therefore difficult, if not impossible, for the unorthodox to gain recognition and respectability. But we know there are energies and vibrations in existence which are difficult to measure and verify in material terms but are recognised and in daily use by those sensitive to their reality. The dilemma facing us as we enter the new millennium, is how to bring science and unorthodoxy together for the good of mankind. Perhaps part of the answer lies in recognising that there is room for both in a world which itself is always changing and evolving.

All humanity is on a spiritual pathway, and whilst many have need for an organisation and brotherhood within which to practise their beliefs, others progress through introspection and faith, but in so doing may be regarded as mistaken or heretic and bring disrepute upon themselves. There are many pathways to the Universal God and every soul will progress at his own speed and in his own time according to his spiritual understanding.

I find it hard to envisage that the way forward towards a better, peaceful and enlightened world will be by the way of orthodox religion. These powerful organisations stifle and discourage freedom of expression and bind their followers with a formalised creed.

Mankind is divided when any one religion claims to have a monopoly of the Divine and Ultimate Truth. Whilst all believe in a supreme deity or deities, divisions exist not only between major religions, but also between sects within those religions. The stronger the religious movement, the greater the chasm between it and all others, and the more fanatical its fundamentalists. This is a truism, but is not meant to devalue the invaluable community and social work carried out by individuals in chapels, churches, synagogues and mosques. Neither does it belittle the spiritual strength and upliftment experienced by members of those organisations.

The world today is a battlefield in which genocide, ethnic cleansing and other hideous crimes are perpetrated in the name of religion and materialism. Only when fundamentalism is put aside and tolerance of others' beliefs is manifest, will religions and churches be able to put aside their differences and come together without bigotry or hatred. Such tolerance and respect for others would bring greater understanding of the nature of God and the nature of man. Only then will peace and harmony prevail. Some time in the not too distant future, there will be a catalyst for such reformation, but in the here and now we need to be aware that our individual spiritual progression is as important to the world's condition, as each drop of water is to the ocean. The purity of each droplet contributing to the quality of the whole. Individual thought is a powerful force and the significant factor in collective thought and the subsequent actions of thousands, if not millions, of others.

Catastrophic disasters that plague the earth have trebled in recent decades. We have seen climatic changes, drought, floods and high loss of lives due in large measure, to global warming and our use of fossil fuels and deforestation. It is the generations since the First World War who have been most unthinking, wasteful and destructive. We should recognise that we exist on a living planet where, without interference, nature is carefully balanced although the planet itself is continuously erupting and changing.

There is no way forward and nothing to be gained by blaming God for our thoughtlessness and greed. We each have a personal responsibility to play our part in preserving the planet's natural resources. It will be the strength of our individual thoughts added to the strength of similar thoughts of others, that will combine to make a collective force for good.

It has long been my belief that led by prophets, teachers and messiahs, the worlds great religions each teach facets of the same Whole Truth, which in its entirety would be beyond our understanding. It is tragic that we all worship the Universal God, but are misled into also worshipping the Messengers. Can it really be that the prophets, teachers and messiahs sought to be worshipped or sanctified? Their teachings suggest they were humble in spirit and did not glorify themselves, except to ask that their followers should heed the teachings they brought. Did not Jesus exhort his followers to "Love the Lord your God with all your heart and with all your soul and with all your mind." He did not seek divinity for himself as he went on, "This is the first and greatest commandment. And the second is like it: Love your neighbour as yourself. All the Law and the Prophets hang on these two commandments."

Within these simple sentences is the affirmation that every living person is able to direct his love to God without the need for an intermediary. We are being asked to stay our hearts and minds upon God and God alone. Importantly, not only should we respect our neighbour as being worthy of our love, that is all mankind irrespective of colour or race, but we should also love ourselves. This can be overlooked, but does it not mean that we should recognise our spirituality and value and nurture our true spiritual self and the Big I that I Am?

When we appreciate and accept the true, eternal nature of our being, we will have found the reason for our pathway through this brief life. With this understanding will come the inspiration to take responsibility for our thoughts and actions, and live our lives in such a way that our spiritual progression in this world will lead to advancement and further progression in the next.